Tika,
Be blessed &
Changed for life!
T.D. Banks
Prov 31:10

A Woman Any Man Can Love

T.D. Banks

Bloomington, IN Milton Keynes, UK
authorHOUSE®

AuthorHouse™
1663 Liberty Drive, Suite 200
Bloomington, IN 47403
www.authorhouse.com
Phone: 1-800-839-8640

AuthorHouse™ UK Ltd.
500 Avebury Boulevard
Central Milton Keynes, MK9 2BE
www.authorhouse.co.uk
Phone: 08001974150

First published by AuthorHouse 2/6/2007

ISBN: 978-1-4259-7257-8 (sc)

Library of Congress Control Number: 2006910977

Printed in the United States of America
Bloomington, Indiana

This book is printed on acid-free paper.

SPECIAL ACKNOWLEDGEMENTS

Thank you to everyone who has been supportive of me with prayer and those who encouraged me with words of kindness. I would like to extend a very special thank you to my sister-in-law, Patricia Doster. Pat, I truly appreciate you giving your time and input on this project. You helped me more than you know.

Also, I would like to thank every individual who believed in the strength of what God deposited within me and contributed financially to ensure that this book would be published in due season.

With great humility, thank you to:

Pastor Anthony Banks – Changed for Life Outreach Ministries
Apostle William Glover – Mt. Hermon Ministries
Bishop Michael Kirk – Ind. Church Fellowship Conference International
Apostle Billy Lubansa "Papa Billy" – Flaming Fire of God Ministries
Mr. Bernard McPherson
Mr. and Mrs. Vincent & Carolyn Brown
Mrs. Vevline McCullum
Mrs. Mildred Williams
Mrs. Barbara Rhone
Ms. Tamika Bellamy
Miss Chante Mariah Robinson
Mrs. Harriet Turner
Mrs. Mattie Johnson
Mrs. Gina Lewis-Sheard
Mr. and Mrs. Kenny & Joyce Campbell
The Daymon Family
Mr. and Mrs. James and Kim Chaney
Healthy Choice Misitries, Inc.

DEDICATION

A Woman Any Man Can Love is my first book and is very near and dear to my heart. However, it pales in comparison to how near and dear my husband of nine years is to my heart. I dedicate this book, my first book to my mighty man of valor, Pastor Anthony Banks. It is such a blessing to have a husband who is such a strong source of support and encouragement. Thank you for the gentle nudges, the hard sayings, and the swift kicks when I wasn't motivated to get up and keep moving. We have seen each other through some trying times and have weathered many storms together. I consider it an honor to share my life with you, to raise our children with you, to do God's work with you, and to continue to mature and grow with you.

I would also like to dedicate this book to my children: Anthony, Toniesha, Loren, and LeNavince (a.k.a. Buddy). Thank you for being patient and understanding for all of the "just 10 more minutes" responses that often turned to 30 more minutes or an hour. I love each of you very much and I pray that you boys will find your virtuous woman when the time is right. I pray that you girls will come forth as the virtuous women that God has equipped you to be.

To my mother, who I have not always agreed with and could not wait to get away from as a teenager— You are literally, my best friend. I appreciate you more now than I ever could have growing up. As we kept the grandkids coming, you continued to be a source of help, encouragement and support for us. It would have been very difficult for us to do what we do without you *and* Vincent. Thank you for everything that you have done for me and continue to do for our family.

I could not have done this without any of you. You are a family that any woman can love!

TABLE OF CONTENTS

PREFACE

There are many fine books on the market concerning the spiritual growth and development of women. This book takes a passage of scripture that is often misconstrued and misunderstood and breaks it down into easily digestible parts so that women can really understand the text and begin to apply its principles to their lives.

While it is not my intention to badger men, the fact remains that a large number of men have not taken their rightful place as priests of their home. There are men who have abandoned, used, and abused their women. Therefore, many women (regardless of race or age) have no desire to pattern their lives after the Proverbs 31 woman and relate her lifestyle as a benefit for a man and not themselves.

Further, this passage has been misrepresented by many very well-meaning preachers. So much so that the attitude of most women concerning the Proverbs 31 woman tends to be, "I hate this woman," rather than, "I want to be this woman."

Women need to recognize that no matter how circumstances appear in their lives, they are full of power. When we allow ourselves to be transparent, realize our shortcomings, and be willing to submit to the process of true change, we become empowered in our emotions, body, and spirit. When this occurs, the fruit of the flesh no longer has a place to abide. Then we can unite, spiritually and emotionally intact, to do what God told Eve in Genesis 3, to produce seed that would crush the enemy's head.

A Woman Any Man Can Love was not written for the purpose of turning women into man magnets or to give them unbelievable sex appeal. I wrote this book for the purpose of educating and empowering others to become a woman that can get God's attention, His favor, and to walk in the destiny that God intends. In the process of becoming the woman that God honors, there is an immeasurable force that can be tapped into. This force will propel women forward to the place they need to be in order to receive whatever it is that God has in store, whether it is a ministry, a career, or a man.

Please know that I do not claim to be the perfect wife, mother, or woman. I recognize that I, too, am a work in progress. So everywhere I use the word "you" throughout this book, it also means "me".

By applying the principles of this book, you will begin a transformation into a woman of grace that any man can love, meaning:

- A wife that any husband can praise.
- A mother that any child can celebrate.
- An employee any boss can appreciate.
- A friend that anyone can enjoy.
- And, a woman who is respected by everyone who knows her.

INTRODUCTION

I heard a message at a New Year's Eve Service several years ago and the minister's subject was titled, "Are you who you say you are?"

It wasn't until the next day that I really began to think about that question and asked myself the following questions:

- *Am I who I say I am?*
- *Do I practice what I preach?*
- *Am I a living example?*
- *Does God look on my life and say, 'That's my virtuous daughter'?*

It's easy to say you're one thing or another. However, if you take the time to examine yourself, are you *really* who you proclaim to be? Do your actions line up with who you *say* you are?

We all have different gifts, areas of expertise, aspirations, and struggles. Nonetheless, we should all strive to be virtuous women of God. It doesn't matter if you are married, single, mother of many, or childless. Living a life that is pleasing in the eyes of God should not be considered as something for older people, married people, or reserved for parents and grandparents. All of God's children are called to righteousness and holiness.

> **Who can find a virtuous woman? For her price is far above rubies.**
> *(Proverbs 31:10)*

The virtuous woman of Proverbs 31 continues to be the topic of much discussion in many circles. Some think she did not possess all of the attributes listed in Proverbs 31. Instead, they believe that they are a collection of attributes that women should strive for. The general consensus of women tends to be: *"No one can do all of that!"*

However, I believe that this woman the Bible speaks of possessed all of the attributes listed in Proverbs 31:10-31. They are both attainable and achievable to incorporate into your life.

A friend of mine preached a message once and discussed what he calls, "Buffet Christianity". He said that many times Christians pick and choose which spiritual principles they will follow and which ones they will not, as if they are in a buffet line.

Now, imagine going into a cafeteria and God is the server on the other side of the buffet line. It would be like saying to God, "Give me a large serving of good health, super-sized financial prosperity, that godly man over there, a little bit of righteousness, some holiness (but not too much). Okay, that's all for now. If I need anything else, I'll send someone to come back for it later."

God does not operate that way. You will never experience the fullness of God's love for you by picking and choosing which commands and spiritual principles you will and will not abide by. It is only when you fully commit your mind, body, and spirit to the Lord that you can have an intimate relationship with Him and be positioned to receive whatever it is that He has for you. If you are going to live a successful Christian life, it is vital that the word of God be the final authority in everything you do. Even in examining your life and your walk with Him.

I used to have the attitude, "Well, you know…everyone has something!"

That "something" was nothing more than an excuse to continue to do my own thing, live according to my rules, and be my own person. Oh yes, followed by trying to dig MYSELF out of trench after trench. When I did it my way I got my results, which was always a mess.

The rebellion got easier and easier and the trenches got deeper and deeper until I gave up my will and finally surrendered to God. When you do it God's way you get God's results, which is His will manifesting in your life.

If you desire to be the virtuous woman that God has called you to be, it's important to understand what makes the woman in Proverbs 31 so noble and gracious in the eyes of everyone who knew her, even Almighty God. He esteemed her so highly that He honored her life by including her in His wonderful book and by causing her to be blessed and to be a blessing. He has greatness planned for your life as well.

As you read this book, ask the Holy Spirit to help you to see yourself and do whatever is necessary to allow all of the virtue within you to manifest outwardly. It is in you, just waiting to come forth. True, life-lasting change will spring forth when you:

1. Admit to yourself that there is a need for change.
2. Consult with your help, the Holy Spirit, requesting assistance as you go through your transition.
3. Make time to read God's word on issues that are challenging for you.
4. Put into action what God reveals to you during your intimate moments of study, prayer, and communication with Him.
5. Finally, pray earnestly that God will lead you to another woman whom you can trust to confide in and who will give you godly counsel, not popular opinion.

CHAPTER ONE

DO YOU SEE THIS WOMAN?

*"Then He turned to the woman and said to
Simon, 'Do you see this woman?'"*
(Luke 7:44, NKJV)

One afternoon I was watching a woman being interviewed on a talk show. A short video played depicting some of the worst moments of her life. At one time she was married, was raising her children, lived in a nice home, and had a very comfortable life. Her husband walked out on her and shortly after she began to use drugs. She became addicted, and as a result of her lifestyle her children were taken away from her, she lost her job, her home, and her car. She ended up working as a prostitute to support her drug habit. She suffered emotionally and physically. She was beaten many times, stabbed, raped, and almost murdered. Fortunately, for her, she was able to get help and begin a new life.

The audience began to applaud for her as she discussed how she is rebuilding with a good job, her own apartment, and a stable life. The interviewer made the statement that she must be so proud of herself for what she has overcome and the progress she was making. The woman's response was that she was glad that her life was spared and that she had a chance to start over. However, she was unable to fully enjoy her successes because she still felt dirty.

The interviewer then said to the woman, "But you have accomplished so much, you have a new life. Why do you still feel dirty?"

The woman answered by saying, "I buy new clothes and shoes. I get my hair done regularly. I get manicures and pedicures to make me look beautiful, but nothing helps. I do all of these things, but I still feel dirty."

At this point, the interviewer is really stressing how great it was that she was able to change her life and was trying to help her feel better about her accomplishments. She could not understand why this woman was unable to shake the image of her past. She asked her again, "Why do you still feel so dirty?"

"Because I'm all used up," the woman said, as the tears streamed down her face.

I could not stop the tears from rolling down my face as I looked at this precious woman say with such brokenness, "I'm all used up."

Even after the show went off, I could still see her face and hear those words, "I'm all used up."

My heart was heavy and my spirit was grieved because this lovely woman did not realize that she was not used up, she was just beginning. She was oblivious to the fact that there is an awesome ministry within her. Lives can be saved because of her experiences. She had no idea that God wants to use her to be a source of encouragement for others.

> *Your past does not dictate your future, no matter how horrible it was.*

She was correct on one point. All of the clothes, shoes, cars, tangible goods, or spas in the world cannot make you feel better about who you are internally. Sure, there will be some enjoyment and fulfillment initially. But when the novelty wears off, you will be left feeling empty inside. Only the power of Christ can make all things new and cleanse you from the inside out.

After the show ended I began to think about the millions of women who have the same mindset that this woman did and think that they are all used up as well. To think that you are used up is to think that you are useless, worthless, without purpose, and without any capacity to give anything or receive anything.

Before we consider the topic of being a woman of virtue, power, and strength—one that is honored and respected by those around her, let's first do some housecleaning. There is some spiritual housekeeping that needs to take place concerning how you see yourself. If you do not possess a healthy self-image, there is no way that you can view yourself as a woman that *anyone* can love because you can't love, respect, or honor yourself.

Concerning your life and your usefulness to your family, to God, or your community, do you see this woman that you just read about? Now, the circumstances behind the mindset do not have to be the same for you to feel and think like the woman on the talk show. So many people struggle because of guilt and shame due to their pasts. They believe that because they have made mistakes, or have been victimized, that there is nothing that can be done or said to make up for it, so they end up stagnated—mentally and spiritually. If these individuals never receive Christ, accept forgiveness, and forgive themselves, the words, "I'm all used up", could very well end up being a self-fulfilling prophesy. The negativity and negative self-image that comes along with that type of mentality will be crippling.

These are people who would give anything to go back and change the past…rewrite history. We all know that it is impossible to change the past or take back what we say or what we do. Although we cannot change the past, I wish more women embraced the fact that your past does not dictate your future, no matter how horrible it was. As long as there is breath in your body, it is impossible to be all used up. God has a purpose and a plan for your life.

> **"For I know the thoughts that I think toward you, says the Lord, thoughts of peace and not of evil, to give you a future and a hope."**
> ***(Jeremiah 29:11, NKJV)***

Some people believe that because they have done wrong in the past or because bad things have happened to them that God hates them, but scripture says different. God says that He knows what His thoughts are concerning you and there is nothing evil about them. He wants to fulfill purpose in your life. He intends for you to walk in your destiny with hope and assurance.

He will not change His mind concerning that purpose and plan because you have made some mistakes. Psalm 89:34-35 states, "My covenant I will not break, nor alter the word that has gone out of my lips. Once I have sworn by My holiness; I will not lie to David" (NKJV).

In Jeremiah 29:11, the words that came forth from God were, "For I know the thoughts that I think toward you, says the Lord, thoughts of peace and not of evil, to give you a future and a hope."

> *He made the executive decision to make you one of His chosen instruments. You did not get a vote.*

In Psalm 89:34-35, God lets us know that He does not break covenants or alter what He says for any reason. He won't take it back and He does not lie. If He said He has a purpose and plan for your life, full of hope and peace, then that is what He meant. God wants that for you. The Psalm text says that He will not lie to David, but God is no respecter of persons. What applies to David, also applies to you. If God will not lie concerning David, He will not lie concerning you either.

Well, how can you be certain that God has a purpose and plan for your life? The answer is found in Jeremiah 1:5, "Before I formed you in the womb I knew [and] approved of you [as my chosen instrument], and before you were born I separated and set you apart, consecrating you; [and] I appointed you as a prophet to the nations" (Amplified Version).

Before you were even born or formed in your mother's womb, God approved of you. He made the executive decision to make you one of His chosen instruments. You did not get a vote. He chose you. Your approval or the approval of anyone else does not matter because God approved you to be His instrument. Not only that, but God says that He separated you, set you apart and consecrated you. I believe that part of the separation was that He separated you from you. What do I mean by this?

The Bible is clear that God's ways are not our ways and His thoughts are not our thoughts (Isaiah 55:9). How many times have you said these words, "I forgive you, but I can't forget"?
Translation:

> *As a courtesy and to be politically correct, I am saying that I forgive you. However, what you did is burned in my memory and I will never forget it. When I see you, I may greet you with a smile to be polite, but in the back of my mind I will be thinking about what you did. It will stay with me forever.*

That is how man thinks. God, on the other hand, has the ability to separate you from your past, your sin, your indiscretions, and your idiosyncrasies. He does not look at you and see your past. He has set you apart from that. When He looks at you He sees your future, your expected end. God is so wonderful that He separated you from you before you were even born. God knew that mistakes would be made. He knew that you would not always make the right choices. He knew that you would sin, but He still approved of you and finds you worthy to be His chosen instrument.

5

He set you apart in His thoughts concerning you so He could consecrate you. To consecrate means to set apart as holy or to declare sacred for religious use. If God thought about your sins and every mistake you make when He looks on you, there is no way He would be able to approve of you. He had to set you apart, so He could view you as holy and sacred.

Jeremiah 1:5 goes on to say, "I appointed you as a prophet to the nations" (Amplified Version). The word prophet means a person inspired by God. A prophet is someone who yields themselves to do what God says they should do, go where God says they should go, and say what God tells them to say. They are guided by the influence of the Holy Spirit. God wants to use you to affect the nations. In the Hebrew, the word nations is translated as foreigner; heathen; Gentile.

God wants to use you to affect those that are foreign to Him and His word. God wants to use you to be His mouthpiece to tell others about His goodness and His grace. God wants you to yield to Him so He can use your life, your experiences, and your past as an instrument to bring hope and encouragement to the lives of others and win souls to Christ. So, you see--it is impossible for you or anyone else to be all used up. God's word cannot be wrong. He has chosen you for His purpose, which will usher you into a wonderful future.

> *It is impossible for you or anyone else to be all used up.*

It is necessary for you to get rid of the guilt and condemnation that are associated with sin. Romans 8:1 states, "There is therefore now no condemnation to those who are in Christ Jesus, who do not walk according to the flesh, but according to the Spirit" (NKJV). Yet, many believers are unable to receive the forgiveness that is made available because of guilt and condemnation. They can't forgive themselves; therefore, they cannot receive God's forgiveness. Receiving forgiveness is just as simple as receiving salvation. You believe it and you receive it. That is the only requirement for receiving forgiveness: Believe it (because God cannot lie) and receive it (because it is available to you).

The Bible says that there is no condemnation for you. The word condemnation means adverse sentence, verdict, or guilty judgment. There is no guilty verdict that has ever been imposed on you by yourself or anyone else that remains upheld in your life. God has overturned the sin and the sentence. Free your mind of it so you can move forward in what God has in store for you.

Holding on to guilt is like walking around as women did centuries ago with the scarlet letter "A" so that everyone would have knowledge of their indiscretion. It is ever before you in your mind as an attempt to keep you imprisoned and in bondage. God has given you the power to break free through His word, His promise, and His redemptive grace.

One day my daughter brought me a note that she made and had decorated with colored hearts and flowers. The note said:

> *To Mommy,*
>
> *You are the greatest mommy ever. Thank you for bringing me into the world. I love you.*

I smiled at how sweet and thoughtful her note was, and it wasn't 10 seconds from that moment that I had the thought, "Yeah, but what about the two that you didn't bring into the world?"

Prior to my first child being born, I had two abortions. There were two lives that I did not bring into the world. What a slap in the face! The enemy would have just loved for me to stay in that moment and wallow in self-condemnation because I made a terrible mistake in the past. If I had done that, I would have rendered myself useless. The enemy would love for the seed to be planted in my mind and spirit that I am not the best mommy ever because I killed two of my children.

I am so thankful that the word of God is able to quench any fiery dart that the enemy sends in my direction. I am so thankful that God is able to forgive me of my sins and cleanse me from all unrighteousness. I am so thankful that God takes my sins and throws them as far as the east is from the west. I am so glad that despite my faults and weaknesses that God still approves of me, loves me, and chooses to use me. Instead of being paralyzed with guilt, I was set free because of the grace and mercy of God. One day when I get to heaven I will get the pleasure of meeting those two children. You see, according to 2 Corinthians 5:8, to be absent from the body is to be present with the Lord. I am confident that they are present with Him right now and one day I will get to see them.

Do not be dragged or kept in bondage because of the past. You are a child of God and as His child you can cry out to Him when you are distressed, confused, or afraid. You cannot hold on to the past. If you call out to God, the Holy Spirit will come to your aid and be an ever-present reminder of who you are in Christ.

> **But the Comforter (Counselor, Helper, Intercessor, Advocate, Strengthener, Standby), the Holy Spirit, Whom the Father will send in My name [in My place, to represent Me and act on My behalf], He will teach you all things. And He will cause you to recall (remind you, bring to your remembrance) everything I have told you.**
> *(John 14:26 Amplified Version)*

Do not be dragged or kept in bondage because of the past

Luke 7:36-50 tells the story of the sinful woman who went to Simon's house in search of forgiveness for her many sins. The Amplified Bible describes her as a woman who not only made some mistakes; but who also was devoted to sin. Just as you may be devoted to your family, church, or job, she was loyal and true to sin. However, she had a change of heart. We don't get to see her in her sin. Instead, we see her broken and contrite, weeping at Jesus' feet, anointing them, and kissing them. She was engaged in intimate worship.

She could not take her life any more the way that it was. She knew that her sins were many and she was willing to pay any cost and do whatever she had to do in order to rid herself of the guilt and shame associated with the way she was living her life. She wanted forgiveness and a new start. However, Simon did not agree with what was taking place and could not understand why Jesus would allow this sinful woman to approach and touch Him. In Luke 7:44, Jesus asks Simon, "Do you see this woman?"

Not merely with your physical eyes, but do you see her spirit; do you see her heart; do you see her potential? Let's go one step further—do you see her as I see her?

You cannot allow the opinions of other people stop you from moving into what God has for you, from yielding yourself to be His chosen instrument, or from giving Him true worship because "they" know about your past mistakes. God will deal with them, just as Jesus dealt with Simon. It does not matter how others see you. What is important is how God sees you.

Jesus asks Simon, "Do you see this woman?" The word "this" is very specific. He didn't say, do you see "a" woman, or "that" woman? He said, "Do you see this woman?" Not just the woman who was at His feet, but the woman in Jeremiah 29:11 that is in the mind of God and has a future and hope. Not just this woman at His feet, but also the woman in Jeremiah 1:5 who God has separated from her past and hand selected as His chosen instrument. Do you see this woman who cares more about living a life free from guilt and shame than she does about what anyone else thinks of her?

After Jesus informs the woman that her faith (what she believed) saved her, He states, "Go, enter into peace in freedom from all the distresses that are experienced as the result of sin" (Luke 7:50, Amplified Version). There are many distresses that are experienced as a result of sin. We lose relationships, we encounter guilt and shame, we miss opportunities, and suffer physically, emotionally, spiritually, and even financially because of sin. Jesus says, it doesn't matter how many or how great your sins are in your mind, they are forgiven. You have to have faith in that and walk in freedom.

Let me ask you a question. When you look at yourself in the mirror of your mind, which woman do you see? Before you can even think about being a woman that anyone wants to be associated with, whether it is a lover, mother, brother, or employer, you have to see "this" woman. Before you can be it, you have to see it. Then, you can live it. Remember it's just like salvation: believe it, receive it, and walk in it. Do you see *this* woman?

FOR YOUR SPIRITUAL GROWTH:

If you suffer from self-condemnation and are carrying guilt from your past, I would like you to do the following exercise when you begin to feel the weight of the distresses associated with sin. Stand in front of a mirror and look at yourself. Don't focus on your features, flaws, or physical imperfections. Begin to look for "this" woman. Look past the make-up (or lack of). Look beyond past hurt, pain, and disappointment. Look for what God sees in His spiritual mind.

This may be difficult to do initially because some wounds run deep. If you are going to build your faith to walk in forgiveness and freedom, then you need to speak faith concerning what God has already spoken concerning you. I don't mean read it or think about it. You need to speak it verbally. Your words are powerful. The power of life and death are in the tongue, so speak life so that "this" woman can emerge. You need to say it, so the words can flow from your mouth, through your ears, and into your heart and spirit. Look at yourself and say the following (and mean it):

> *"I am God's chosen instrument. God has set me apart and*
> *declared me sacred and holy to be used by Him. I am full*
> *of potential, hope, and I have a future. God has a purpose*
> *and a plan for my life. He has already forgiven me and*
> *I receive that forgiveness. I am free from the physical <u>and</u>*
> *mental bondage of sin. Use me Lord. I yield myself to you*
> *God as a prophet to the nations."*

CHAPTER TWO

WHAT IS A VIRTUOUS WOMAN?

"A virtuous woman, who can find? Her price is far above rubies."
Proverbs 31:10

What do you think of when you hear the word virtuous? What exactly does it mean to be virtuous? The persona of a virtuous woman has been misrepresented by both men and women. There are those that believe a virtuous woman is a wife and mother that pleases her husband's every need and cares for her children with love and great ease. Some believe a virtuous woman is a woman who loves God and is perfect in every way. Still, others believe a woman of virtue is one who is mature in age and settled in life. All of these beliefs are partly true, but neither reflects the true meaning of a virtuous woman.

Additionally, being a woman any man can love goes beyond the exterior. As a matter of fact, being a woman any man can love has nothing to do with the clothes you wear, your hairstyle, the car you drive, your dress size or career path. You can be as beautiful as Halle Berry and as curvatious as Beyonce Knowles, and suffer a nervous breakdown at the slightest sign of adversity. You can be as rich and powerful as Oprah Winfrey, but lack good morals and integrity. Being a woman any man can love has nothing to do with money, sex, or power. Instead, she is a woman who commands God's ear, His favor, and is clothed with strength and honor.

> **"Strength and honor are her clothing; and she shall rejoice in time to come."**
> ***(Proverbs 31:25)***

In the next two to three chapters we are going to go to school.

The subject: The Virtuous Woman
The textbook: The Bible
The main text: Proverbs 31:10-31

I will give you a lot of definitions pertaining to this passage of scripture. In deciding to write this book it was important to me not to fill the pages with a lot of "feel good" statements and no explanations. Just hang in there for a chapter or two, I promise that there will be plenty to shout about later!

So, to begin answering the question, "What is a virtuous woman?" we will begin with what God says concerning the infamous woman in Proverbs 31. Proverbs 29:18 states, "Where there is no vision [no redemptive revelation of God], the people perish" (Amplified Version).

It is important to understand what God is revealing through His word. It is in the revelation of God's word that we receive redemption and true life. Without redemption we remain spiritually dead. It is important to have a clear understanding of what the Bible is communicating to us so we can be what Jesus says in Matthew 10:16, "as wise as serpents, and as harmless as doves" concerning our lives, the decisions that must be made, and the actions that we must take.

> **"Who can find a virtuous woman? For her price is far above rubies."**
> ***(Proverbs 31:10)***

The Hebrew word for virtuous means a force, whether of men, means, or other resources. It comes from a word that means to twist or whirl in a circular or spiral manner. This force is a spiraling force.

Think for a moment about a tornado. It is a force that is generated through resources in nature. There are certain times when conditions in the environment are favorable for a tornado to develop. When these conditions are present, a tornado develops and begins to travel on a certain course. It is not easy to know ahead of time the

> *The Hebrew word for virtuous means a force, whether of men, means, or other resources.*

path that a tornado will take. Meteorologists know when the conditions are favorable and where one is likely to develop, but the path is not predictable.

Not only is the word virtuous defined as a force, but another definition for virtuous is, army. Just like a tornado, certain resources also perpetuate armies. A few examples are intelligence, sophisticated weaponry, troops, and finances. When these resources are used wisely and commands are followed with precision, an army should be able to conquer any adversary. Therefore, our description of a virtuous woman is as follows:

> A virtuous woman is one who possesses a strong spiritual force with the pattern and strength of a tornado. God created her to develop into a woman full of strength. Once she is fully developed, she is well on her way to fulfilling her destiny. Others cannot predict her exact path. It may appear that she is moving about haphazardly, but she is tuned in to the voice of God and following His direction. Her power is likened unto a full-scale army. Through her resources of prayer, fasting, studying God's word and wearing His whole armor, she is able to go into spiritual battle with tornado-like winds, the force of an army, and come out victorious!

This is the woman God has created you to be. This is the power God has already equipped you with. The force of a tornado and the power of an army are intertwined and wrapped up inside of you. You don't have to wait for it to come to you. You already possess it. The only thing required of you is to operate in it.

Unfortunately, as women, we experience varying degrees of tragedy and misfortune in our lives. Whether it is unstable parental relationships, bad marriages, horrific divorces, problems with raising children, sexuality, or abortion, all of it is tragic. These negative experiences often times leave us spiritually wounded and feeling power-less when God created us to be power-full.

It is a deception from Satan to make you feel like you have no power, when the truth of the matter is that you have ALL of the power. If he can make you think and feel that you are under control and not in control, then he wins. What you need to remember is what God has said about you.

> **And the LORD shall make thee the head, and not the tail; and thou shalt be above only, and thou shalt not be beneath; if that thou hearken unto the commandments of the LORD thy God, which I command thee this day, to observe and to do them: (Deuteronomy 28:13).**

However, there are some requirements on your part. The next verse states, "And thou shalt not go aside from any of the words which I command thee this day, to the right hand, or to the left, to go after other gods to serve them" (Deuteronomy 28:14).

God is prepared to open up the windows of heaven and pour out blessings upon you. God is prepared to give you the (right) desires of your heart. God is prepared to exalt you and make your name great, however, you have to be obedient to His word and serve Him only. It is only through following the leading and guidance of the Holy Spirit that you can have the fullness of God's blessings and that you can overcome the past so that emotional and spiritual healing can occur.

We all have scars and have been wounded in many areas, not just physically, but spiritually and emotionally as well. Too often, when this happens, women are deemed unworthy by the standards of the world, the church, and also by themselves. In the face of such adversity and self-condemnation, some have a tendency to withdraw from the Lord at the very time that they should be pressing and forcing their way into His presence. God has called you to be a mighty force to be reckoned with in His kingdom.

The time has come for you to rise and become the virtuous woman that God has called you to be and begin to restore what the enemy has stolen by utilizing your spiritual resources. Remember what is written in Jeremiah 1:5, "Before I formed you in the womb I knew [and] approved you [as my chosen instrument], and before you were born I separated and set you apart, consecrating you; [and] I appointed you as a prophet to the nations" (*Amplified Bible*).

Before you were born, before you committed your first sin, before you told your first little white lie, before you made what you thought was the biggest mistake of your life, God had already selected you to do great and mighty things. He has a purpose and a plan for your life that does not have to be cancelled because you've made some mistakes. God made a provision for sin, His Son Christ. God's purposes and plans do not stop because you fall. He still wants to use you. Ask for forgiveness, but more importantly, receive the forgiveness, pick yourself up and keep moving forward.

Receiving forgiveness is difficult for many people, but its really rather simple. It's funny how we receive salvation and walk in that belief, but when it comes to receiving forgiveness from the same person who gave us salvation, there is a dilemma. Remember, receiving forgiveness is just as easy as it is to receive salvation. The only requirement is to believe. Believe that God has forgiven you, forgive yourself, and keep putting one foot in front of the other. I have heard women say, "I believe that God has forgiven me, but I can't forgive myself."

My response is always the same, "Are you greater than God?"

15

Think about it. The creator of heaven and earth casts our sins into the sea of forgetfulness and says come to me and I will give you rest. How can you not enter into the peace and safety that your Heavenly Father provides?

Who can find a virtuous woman?

Proverbs 31:10 asks the question, "Who can find a virtuous woman?"

This is a two-fold question. The word "find" means to acquire. It also means to come forth. Not only is Proverbs 31:10 asking who can acquire a virtuous woman, but also, what woman can come forth as virtuous? In order for a virtuous woman to be found, she first has to come forth or present herself as virtuous.

Sometimes women can be a little *too* harsh in passing judgment on men with statements like, "There just aren't any good men out there anymore."

Could it be that there is a decrease in the number of women presenting themselves as virtuous? Men experience emotional hurt at the hands of women just as women experience hurt from men. This is not to excuse the behavior of men who treat women poorly. However, in many instances, when a man does not honor and respect women, the root cause of it stems from a woman in his life (lover, mother, sister, aunt, friend, etc.) who did not present herself as a woman of virtue.

Another example is in the marketplace. How many times have you heard an unemployed person say, "There's just no good jobs out there"?

That is absurd! There are hundreds and thousands of "good jobs" available. The question becomes, is that person qualified to satisfy the job requirements? Have they come forth as a viable job candidate?

Here's another good one. "I don't trust any of those church people.

They're all phony and the preacher is just out to get money."

Again, it's not that there are no good churches to get plugged into and receive the word of God. Just like the previous scenarios, has this person come forth as trustworthy, open, and honest? Have they come forth with their time, talents, and resources to make improvements that will better the church?

So, in order for a virtuous woman to be found, she must first come forth as virtuous. The last clause of verse 10 says, "her price is far above rubies". Who can acquire her, for her price is far above rubies? What man can attain her because her price is far above rubies? What employer can hire and retain her because her price is far above rubies? What church can disciple and feed her, for her price is far above rubies?

> *Proverbs 31:10 asks the question, "Who can find a virtuous woman?"*

What is it that makes a virtuous woman so valuable? Her value is connected to her favor with God. Proverbs 18:22 says, "Whoso findeth a wife findeth a good thing and obtaineth favor of the Lord." The Message Bible states it this way, "Find a good spouse, you find a good life—and even more: the favor of God!"

Single women, stay with me; you're not left out. There is a qualifier that makes any woman eligible for this favor—married or single. The qualifier is found in the word, "find" or "findeth".

You see, the word "findeth" in this verse is the same Hebrew word for "find" that is in Proverbs 31:10. This statement is also two-fold. The Bible is saying whoever attains a true wife, attains a good thing and obtains favor of the Lord. The scripture is also saying, whoever comes forth as a true wife also, comes forth as a good thing and obtains favor of the Lord.

So, if you are single, do not discount or eliminate yourself from this favor because the word "wife" is used. Additionally, Proverbs 18:22 states, "find a good spouse". When you are found you're not married, you're single. You have to first be found good and true. In other words, come forth as good and true and you too will obtain the same favor of the Lord.

I have often heard this verse used as a measuring stick for men to look out for the right woman. To stop there leaves out the other side of the coin, which is for women to come forth as virtuous (full of power, strength, and grace) so that they too, can obtain favor of the Lord. So, what is this favor that can be obtained?

The word favor in this verse means delight, especially <u>as shown</u>. The word favor originates from a word in the Hebrew that means delight, <u>specifically to satisfy a debt</u>. In Proverbs 18:22, the word "obtaineth" means to secure. Not only to secure, but figuratively it also means *to succeed*. Replacing the original text with these definitions, it would read:

> *Whoever comes forth as a virtuous woman, comes forth as a good thing and secures delight and success from the Lord.*

Psalms 35:27 tells us what brings God delight, "The Lord takes pleasure in the prosperity of His servants." The Lord wants to satisfy your debts for you, whether they are physical, spiritual, financial, emotional or relational debts. He wants you to experience prosperity in every area of your life.

Do you have insufficient funds to pay off the various debts in your life? Have you acquired some bad habit, attitude, or pattern of behavior that you can't seem to get rid of? If this is the case, you need to come forth as the virtuous woman that God has called you to be and go boldly to His throne of grace where you can find favor, some demonstrated delight, in your time of need.

A time of need is just that, a time that you need God to demonstrate

His love for you by doing something for you, no matter what that "something" is. But please not that it is not necessary to wait until a "time of need" for God to do something special and unique in your life. You are a daughter of Almighty God and a joint heir with Christ, your Redeemer. You shouldn't have to wait until you're in a jam and then call on God. Come forth as a virtuous woman now and watch the favor of God manifest in your life. Not because you're in a crisis, but simply because He is pleased with you for humbling and submitting yourself to Him.

If you are married, you not only set yourself up for favor from God, but you also put your husband in a position to be blessed by God. You will see this in subsequent chapters. Many married women complain about what their partner in life *is not*. Could it be that they, (the wives) have not come forth as virtuous?

Do you realize that you could be the stumbling block in your spouse's life? You, not the devil, could be his worst enemy. Proverbs 31:12 states, "She will do him good and not evil all the days of his life." Pray for your husband, that the will of God (not yours) be done in his life. Encourage and uplift him. Be supportive of him. And when he needs it, be willing to give him the space he needs.

Proverbs 12:2 says, "A good wife is a crown to her husband, but a wicked one is as rottenness to his bones." Choose to be a blessing, not a curse. Come forth, virtuous wife.

If you are single, come forth as virtuous while you are single so God can demonstrate His delight in you by giving you the mate He intends for you to have. It is also important for you to understand that virtue is not tied to gender, one of the definitions for virtuous is *valor*.

Position yourself to receive your mighty man of valor. The Bible says that one can put a thousand to flight, and two will put ten thousand to flight. If it is your desire to get married, start out with an advantage over the enemy. The best mate is not the one with the best car, the best job, the best house, the most money, and definitely not the best looks. He is the one that God wills for you to have.

Whatever your occupation may be, come forth as virtuous so God can elevate you and bless you in your career. When you are positioned properly your company or organization will thrive because of your virtue, because you have favor with God, and because you have resources that extend beyond finances.

If you are a mother, come forth as virtuous so God can show you how to be wise in your decision-making concerning your children. He wants to be a blessing to you so you can, in turn, bless them.

Whether you are married, looking to get married, content in your singleness, employed in or outside of the home—breaking out of self-constructed molds and those of society in order to walk in the power that God has given you will set you up for continued success. So, first seek the Kingdom of God (His way of doing things) and every desire that lines up with His will for your life will be added unto you.

FOR YOUR SPIRITUAL GROWTH

I want to close this chapter with some key concepts that you can begin to incorporate in your life as you strive to become the virtuous woman that God has called you to be.

- True Repentance: For change to take place, you must first recognize that there is a problem. Once the problem is identified, whether it is a trespass of omission or commission, it is necessary to repent. True repentance is not merely asking for forgiveness, but it results in a change of behavior and a change in the opposite direction.

- Use Spiritual Weapons: The virtuous woman's resources are her spiritual weaponry. We are not fighting against flesh and blood; this is a spiritual battle. It doesn't do any good to battle people. Take it to the next level and begin to fight in the spirit realm with the weapons that God has given you. You will waste time and energy fighting people. People aren't your enemy or the source of your problems. The battle is in the spirit. It is vital that you become a woman of prayer. Get in the habit of communicating with God. And remember, communication is a two-way conversation. It's important to spend time listening. You will not recognize the voice of God if you don't spend time studying His word. Don't just study, but begin to make application of the word. Fasting is another powerful spiritual weapon that gets results. Study Isaiah 58. It gives insight to improper motives for fasting and what the Lord deems as proper fasting. Isaiah 58:6 gives the reason God has chosen for fasting, "to loose the chains of injustice and untie the cords of the yoke, to set the oppressed free and break every yoke." Verses 8-14 state what the rewards and blessings of fasting are. Remember, there are many ways one can fast. You don't necessarily have to fast for long periods of time. You can fast a meal, a day, a week, etc. The choice is yours. Just try and keep your commitment. (*If you have a medical condition, always check with your physician before making a decision to fast.*)

• Finally, <u>consult God.</u> Before making decisions, no matter how small, consult God. Let the word of God be the final authority in your life. Many situations could be avoided if you would ask God first and be receptive to the leading of the Holy Spirit. Keep Matthew 6:33 in the forefront of your thinking, "But seek ye first the Kingdom of God, and His righteousness; and all these things shall be added unto you."

In the next chapter we will look at how the virtuous woman is not hasty in her decision-making, but takes the time to carefully plan. Virtuous woman, are you who you say you are? Examine yourself.

CHAPTER THREE

CAPTURING THE HEART

"The heart of her husband doth safely trust in her, so that he will have no need of spoil." Proverbs 31:11

The Amplified Bible states, "He will have no need of unrighteous gain or lack of righteous gain" (Proverbs 31:11). The center of his being and everything within him trusts in her. He has complete confidence in her. Although this section deals with the confidence a husband has in his wife, this can also be applied to an employer, a ministry head, or anyone you are connected to.

Those that we are in relationship with and are joined to spiritually should be able to have trust and confidence in us as virtuous women. Whoever and whatever we are connected to should reap the benefits of being connected to a virtuous woman. So as you read this chapter, do not think only in terms of the husband-wife relationship. Also, consider those that you are joined and connected to spiritually, professionally, and personally.

The thought of a husband having so much confidence in his wife was intriguing for me. There have been times when I mentioned something to my husband or did some things that made him look at me sideways. So, how is it that the husband of the virtuous woman can have so much assurance in her? Let's look at a few examples.

> *He knows that she makes wise decisions and weighs out options before acting.*

First, she has a proven track record. Proverbs 31:16 says, "She considereth a field and buys it; from her profits she plants a vineyard" (*NIV*). The virtuous woman is a planner. The verse says she considers (plans or purposes) then she buys it. She's not impulsive in her decision-making and doesn't go off "half-cocked" making haphazard decisions. She takes the time to evaluate the situation and possibly explores other options before making a concrete decision. Her husband can have a high level of confidence in her because he knows that she makes wise decisions and weighs out options before acting.

When I have to make a decision to do something, my natural inclination is to act now and think later. If I am convinced that it is something that I absolutely need to do, and if I think my husband or someone else may not be in agreement, it hastens my actions because I WANT TO DO IT. This is an area that God has had to deal with me on because I do not like to wait and become impatient when I believe it is something important or vital. When these situations occur I go through a mental process of what I should do versus what I am actually going to do, and most of the time it ends badly. It is at that time when the words of my mother echo in my head, "When you know better, do better!"

What I have learned is that if there is some pressure to make a quick decision on something and the other party or situation cannot wait, it is probably best to let the opportunity pass you by. It will seem as if you are losing out, but in retrospect, you will see that it was a good decision not to act so quickly. It is a terrible feeling to get involved, accept terms, or obligate yourself too quickly, and later want to kick yourself because whatever you agreed to becomes something you want to get out of, but can't. So, before making decisions, make sure you take the time to consult God, consider your options, and carefully evaluate the situation.

She considers, she buys, and she plants. The virtuous woman is methodical. She sees things through to completion. She has a purpose for her tasks, activities, and acquisitions. She invests in what she acquires in such a way that her acquisitions continue to be a blessing for her and her family and those connected to her.

As much as it is important to be a good steward of your money and of your tangible assets, it is equally, (if not more), important to invest wisely in the people that God places around you. Even God Almighty uses people to accomplish His will for His children. We're no different. There are several ways you can invest in someone. You can invest time, knowledge, and expertise. You can invest financially. You can even invest prayer (as incense going up to the nostrils of God as a sweet-smelling fragrance). All of these are types of investments that have the potential of catching root and producing much more fruit in your life, as well as the lives of others.

When you act wisely, you will make wise decisions. Ask God to give you wisdom in your daily decision-making. Consider the following passages of scripture:

> **If any of you is deficient in wisdom, let him ask of the giving God [Who gives] to everyone liberally *and* ungrudgingly, without reproaching *or* faultfinding, and it will be given him.**
> *(James 1:5 Amplified Version)*

> **For the Lord gives skillful *and* godly Wisdom; from His mouth come knowledge and understanding.**
> *(Proverbs 2:6 Amplified Version)*

When you incorporate that wisdom into your life, you will be able to plant the same wisdom into the life of someone else.

> **She opens her mouth in skillful and godly wisdom, and on her tongue is the law of kindness [giving counsel and instruction].**
> *(Proverbs 31:26 Amplified Version)*

James 1:5 lets us know that God will give skillful and godly wisdom to anyone who asks for it. Then, in Proverbs 31:26, we see the virtuous woman *giving* skillful and godly wisdom. She consults God in the affairs of her life and receives wisdom in how to make decisions. You need to do the same thing. You can drive yourself crazy going to person after person after person to find out how to handle a situation when God gives skillful wisdom and instruction. This is not to say don't seek the advice of others, just be cautious when you are looking for answers. Do not allow just *anyone* to give you advice. Remember that not everyone will have your best interest at heart or know what is in line with God's will for your life. My advice, seek God first in everything. He will even lead you to the person who has proper counsel for you and your situation.

A lot of well-meaning women give horrible advice that comes from the School of Hard Knocks. Yes, Hard Knocks. The advice they give knocked them down when they used it, but because they do not know the right thing to do (or don't want to see you succeed in life) they tell you what they did. What they don't tell is how their decisions affected them negatively and how they are probably still suffering because of those decisions.

Be careful when it comes to giving and receiving counsel. Be certain that the one you are receiving from receives from the Holy Spirit. Also, be certain that the counsel you give comes from the Holy Spirit. Let the Holy Spirit lead and guide you. Others may not necessarily know how you always come out on top when some circumstances appear to be a no win situation. They may not understand why situations work out best for you in the long run. However, your husband, children, boss, or close friends will come to the place where they recognize that there is something uniquely different about you. They will trust you and your decisions from their heart, the center of their being because you will have a proven track record.

Does this happen immediately? Of course not. Begin now to consult God and evaluate before acting. If you have had an issue with making bad decisions it will take time for others to trust you openly and willingly. Just like everything else in life, it takes time to establish and re-establish trust. But, be patient and let God continue to perfect you. If you are obedient, patient, and remain on the potter's wheel, you will see the difference in your life and begin to capture the hearts of those that matter and mean the most to you.

FOR YOUR SPIRITUAL GROWTH

For all of the activities, acquisitions, groups and people that you are attached to or you are considering becoming attached to you need to think about the following:

1. Sincerely think about the advantages and disadvantages of your involvement and the affect(s) that your association will have on your family or others in your circle of influence. This will let you know if it will be a wise use of your time, talent, and/or finances. Be honest with yourself, use the Word as the final authority and act accordingly.

2. After evaluating, if your decision is to move forward with it, begin to ask yourself:

    "How can I affect this (whatever it is) in a positive way?"

    "What can I bring into this to cause it to grow and prosper?"

    "What from this can I utilize somewhere else to be a blessing?"

3. Lastly, eliminate guilty feelings. Don't allow guilt to set in if you discover that there are activities or associations you have to let go. Just recently I had to do this very thing concerning an area of ministry. Let me just say that it is better to be in the will of God for your life opposed to the belly of a whale. Come when He tells you to come. Stay when He tells you to stay. But, go when He tells you to go.

CHAPTER FOUR

VIRTUOUS WOMAN RISE

*"She riseth also while it is yet night, and giveth meat to
her household, and a portion to her maidens."*
Proverbs 31:15

A woman of virtue is a woman of prayer that gets results. She is actively involved in spiritual battle. The words in Proverbs 31:15 are full of power. Let's examine them carefully.

First, the word "rise" that is used in this verse means to rise, literally or figuratively, and carries the connotation of enduring. The word "night" in this context means a twist away from the light, adversity, or a season of adversity. This is key. Recall the definition of the root word for virtuous: to twist or whirl in a spiral manner. The words virtuous and night are opposing forces.

The virtuous woman's force is spiraling forward to achieve victory, and the "night season" or period of adversity is a twist away from the light to bring loss and destruction. They cannot exist together.

Let me also point out that the verse says she rises "also" while it is night, which is an indication that she is rising (enduring, being steadfast), not only during troubling times, but also when there is peace. It's easy to pray and get in the word when there's a problem. Many of us are forced to at those times, but there's something to be said of the woman that is faithful and remains consistent when nothing is wrong. It's important to plant good seed continually so there will always be a good harvest.

> *A woman of virtue is a woman of prayer that gets results.*

We see that she rises—endures seasons of adversity—but why? She rises to give meat to her household and a portion to her maidens. The word "giveth" in Proverbs 31:15 means, something carried like a ship carrying cargo. A ship carries cargo in its belly from one place to another. The word "meat" is defined in Hebrew as, something torn or spoils. Spoils are goods taken as a result of warfare.

Inserting the meanings to these words into the text, what we have is a woman who endures during periods of adversity and delivers the goods of warfare from the enemy to her household. This is good, but there is more to the act of rising.

Here is how Webster's Dictionary defines rise:

1. *To stand or sit up after sitting, kneeling, or lying*
2. *To rebel; revolt*
3. *To go up; ascend*
4. *To appear above the horizon, as the sun*

The Most High God has a name, El Elyon. The ministry or function of El Elyon is to elevate and resurrect. In other words, His function is to cause you to rise. Deuteronomy 28:1 says, "And it shall come to pass, if thou shalt hearken diligently unto the voice of the Lord thy God, to observe and to do all His commandments which I command thee this day, the Lord thy God will set thee on high above all nations of the earth". When you make God the Most High in your life and receive the ministry of El Elyon, He will raise you up and elevate you.

So if you find yourself flat on your back because you can't handle the pressure of life's problems, you need to call on El Elyon, the Most High God, so He can begin to elevate you and change your posture and ultimately your spiritual position.

If you're sitting down, doing nothing and letting the enemy run your affairs, your marriage, your children, your ministry, your job, STOP IT TODAY! Call on El Elyon, the Most High God, who is well able to equip you for spiritual battle.

> *Just because the enemy brings trouble your way, it does not mean that the trouble will inhabit your life.*

To you who've been on your knees diligently praying, it's time to rise and rejoice! Once you have been diligent in praying, standing on the word (observing to do), and are in compliance and good standing with the Lord, rise! There comes a time when you need to get up off of your knees and begin to rejoice, worship, praise God, and thank Him for answered prayer BEFORE you see it manifest with your natural eyes. Whatever state you're in, call on the Most High God so you can rise and go to the next spiritual level.

To rise also means to revolt. The virtuous woman doesn't sit back and let life happen to her. During times of adversity she fights by going into spiritual battle and doesn't cave in under the pressure. She rejects and revolts against what the enemy brings to her.

Now, just because the enemy brings trouble your way, it does not mean that the trouble has to inhabit your life. It may come, but it will not come to rest on you.

Jesus is clear in John 16:33 that in this world we will have trouble. So, trouble will come. After He makes this statement, He lets us know that we do not have to worry about trouble coming because He came to overcome the world and any trouble that may come. Not only that, but Christ is in you. If Christ overcame the troubles of the world, then because He is in you, you too can overcome the trouble that comes your way.

My favorite definition for rise is to appear above the horizon as the sun. In the natural, the horizon is a place of confusion. You can't determine where the sky ends and the earth begins. There isn't a definite point of distinction with the natural eye. It is possible to be in a spiritual position where the things of the world and the things of God have become so intermingled in your mind that you can't distinguish between the two. To you, everything blends together which results in confusion. You start questioning yourself and you don't know the voice of God from the voice of the enemy, and your own thoughts.

This is why you need the power of the Most High God to elevate you and bring you up above those issues and circumstances so you can begin to evaluate the situation from a higher, spiritual vantage point and through the eyes of Christ, the Son. The Most High God can bring you above the horizons in your life—places of confusion—so you can see them as the Son sees them. Take your heavenly seat with Jesus. The Bible says you are a joint heir with Christ. As a joint heir you have access to the same power, the same anointing, and the same ability that Jesus operated in when He walked the earth.

As a matter of fact, Jesus said that we would do greater things, "Verily, verily, I say unto you, He that believeth on me, the works that I do shall he do also; and greater works than these shall he do; because I go unto my Father" (John 14:12). RISE VIRTUOUS WOMAN!

Secondly, don't let past experiences hinder you from moving up spiritually. Begin to realize that you are not what happened to you, nor are you what you may have done in the past. If you've truly repented (which results in a change of behavior and attitude) and are living a godly life, don't let anyone cause you to operate in self-condemnation. Remember, there is no condemnation, no guilty verdict, or no adverse sentence that has ever been placed on you or that you placed on yourself that applies to you any longer. It doesn't matter how horrible you think it is.

> *Don't let past experiences hinder you from moving up spiritually.*

It is going to take heavy spiritual battle to reclaim your life, your family, and your ministry. These things should not be in the hands of the enemy. They belong to the heirs of Salvation. Restoration is going to require prayer, fasting, studying, praise, worship, giving, humility, sacrifice, forgiving, and loving. Romans 8:28 says, "And we know that all things work together for good to them that love God, to them who are the called according to His purpose." You will have to get out of the buffet line, selecting a few spiritual principles to follow every now and then, and sit down for a ten-course meal!

Proverbs 31:15 goes on to say that after she rises, she "giveth" to her family and her maidens. As previously stated, the word "giveth" means something carried as cargo in the belly of a ship. As a woman, you have the ability to carry a baby in your womb until the time of delivery. To go through delivery means there is some pain involved. To make it through delivery, you may have to grit your teeth, hold on to something, cry, scream, and push with every ounce of strength within you. The same thing applies in spiritual battle. You are going to sweat, and you will experience some pain. You are going to cry, moan, and you may even scream. But once you grab a hold of and embrace that which God intends for you and you see the manifestation in your life, you will look back over the experience and see that it was well worth the fight and you will have a testimony.

Women who have been through delivery often times will get with other women who have either been through delivery, are about to go through it, or are thinking about it. They talk about what labor and delivery was like for them. What a privilege it can be to be able to tell someone else about your spiritual battle and how you had to wait and travail. What an honor, to share your testimony with another about how you held on and kept breathing and pushing until you got the victory.

Remember what the virtuous woman gives to her family, meat, which is defined as spoil (goods taken from the enemy in warfare). What has the enemy taken from you and your family? What is it that you've let slip away? It doesn't belong to him. It belongs to you and your precious loved ones. The Bible says she "giveth meat to her household". She rises, doing all of those necessary acts to be positioned above her circumstances and her life experiences so she can accurately assess the situation with the mind of Christ and enters spiritual battle and takes back what has been stolen!

I have to tell you, it's not just about you. Think of your family, your husband (or husband-to-be), your children, and your children's children. It's also about those people around you, including those under your authority and those who respect you. She not only delivered meat to her family, but also to her maidens. Again, she's investing and imparting into the lives of others.

The Bible asks in, Malachi, "Will a man rob God?" This question is asked in reference to the tithe and offerings. But I ask you, will you rob yourself of the power, the force that God has given you to operate in? Will you rob your family, your husband, your children, your church, or your employer of additional blessings and favor from God? Will you rob those around you of godly wisdom, insight, spiritual and earthly blessings?

Don't spend so much time, energy, and money becoming a strong, independent female and be negligent in becoming a strong and mighty woman of God. As a female, you have so much power. You have favor with God and power over the enemy. The Bible is clear that there would be enmity between the woman and the serpent and the seed of the woman would bruise the serpent's head. What you give birth to, your seed, is powerful enough to stop the devil in his tracks. It is vital that you tap into the awesome power that has been given to you and be in God's perfect will for your life.

It is believed that the most intelligent of human beings only use a small percentage of the brain's capability. I wonder what percentage of the virtue and anointing we use in our lives to accomplish our goals and to fulfill God's destiny in our lives. God absolutely has a purpose and a plan for your life. Many times, that will require moving out of comfort zones, taking off spiritual masks, and breaking free from the traditional acts which cause God's word to be of no effect.

It is the job of the enemy, not so much to attack you, but to attempt to hinder the Kingdom of God. We all have a function in the kingdom, so if he can slow us down or stop us then there is an affect on the kingdom. The Bible says Satan is like a roaring lion. He isn't a roaring lion; he just pretends to be so you'll be fearful and afraid. He's a fraud, a counterfeit, and a defeated foe, a spiritual "wanna-be". Don't be afraid of him, virtuous woman of God. Rise, in every sense of the word. It's time to rise and reclaim everything that you have been robbed of; everything you allowed to slip through your fingers; and everything that God said shall be in your life.

In the last chapter I asked, how is it that the husband and others connected to a virtuous woman can have so much confidence and trust in her? Ultimately, it is because they know that regardless of whatever is going on around her, she will forever rise. What will you do?

FOR YOUR SPIRITUAL GROWTH

When you are striving to make improvements in your life, whether they are physical, mental, or spiritual changes, there are sacrifices that must be made. After reading this chapter you should understand the importance of prayer and how crucial it is to be victorious in spiritual battle. I want to encourage you to start a prayer journal, either on paper or a computer file, so you can be strategic in warfare. Begin by making a list of what you know the enemy has stolen from you, your family, household, etc. In your prayer time call those things, issues, and circumstances out to God and declare restoration and wisdom concerning what you need to do.

1. In your personal study time find examples in scripture of individuals with circumstances similar to yours and learn from what they did (or did not do) during their season of adversity.

2. If God leads you to fast, do it with your list in mind. Study Isaiah 58 to get revelation concerning God's intent and purpose for fasting. During your fast pray continuously and be alert because God will use your time of fasting and everyday occurrences to speak to you and give you direction.

3. Whatever direction God leads you, commit to do whatever He speaks to your spirit. Do not make the mistake that so many make by asking God for wisdom and when He delivers it, you ignore it. Virtuous woman, it's time to rise!

CHAPTER FIVE

THE FRUIT OF YOUR HANDS

"Give her of the fruit of her hands;
and let her own works praise her in the gates."
Proverbs 31:31

The hands are extensions of the arms and are used to perform a variety of functions, mainly holding and grasping. Spiritually speaking, the hands are vital in the lives of believers in their walk and service to the Lord. Think about it. Thanksgiving, praise, worship, prayer, and healing are all acts that require the use of the hands to some degree.

The Bible makes numerous references to the "mighty hand" of God, which indicate power, means (resources), and direction. God's mighty hand delivered many people out of bondage. As an extension of God's mighty hand, Moses parted the Red Sea. God, with His mighty hand, has the ability to take our sinful deeds and remove them from us, "as far as the east is from the west," (Psalms 103:12). Jesus, also an extension of God on earth, accomplished His mission through God's hand, which was with Him. Luke 4:18-19 reads:

"The Spirit of the Lord is upon me, because he hath anointed me to preach the gospel to the poor; he

hath sent me to heal the brokenhearted, to preach deliverance to the captives, and recovering of sight to the blind, to set at liberty them that are bruised, to preach the acceptable year of the Lord."

All of us are extensions of God's mighty hand here on earth. He is mighty and powerful, and He uses us to accomplish His goals. We all have a purpose, a function, and a plan to fulfill that was preordained by Him. We have power!

I want you to take a moment and think about the grand 4th of July fireworks. When that "missile" is lit and it goes soaring into the air, it catches your attention because of the whistling sound it makes. That one streak of light isn't too impressive at first. But the more of it that burns the more explosive it becomes until each individual crystal contained in that missile is ignited, and they all go off in different directions revealing their vivid colors. It is a beautiful display of grand proportion. Each flame is an extension of the main capsule. Even though they come from a main source, they each have power of their own that is fueled by that main source.

Just like that power-packed capsule of gunpowder that contains all the necessary ingredients to result in the display of fireworks, God is also full of power and everything that is needed to accomplish the predestined end is wrapped up in Him. We are extensions of God. By ourselves, we can make some noise and maybe attract some attention. However, if we all "get on fire" and allow ourselves to be used and fueled by the Spirit, there is a glorious display of majesty and a splendid manifestation of God's glory that can occur. This is the type of glory that will cause the unsaved to stop, stare, and seek out more of what Christ has to offer.

As an extension of God's hand, it is vital to make sure that what is produced by your hands (your power, resources,

> *All of us are extensions of God's mighty hand here on earth.*

and direction) has the same, if not <u>more</u> power than that of Jesus Christ. Jesus said, in Luke 14:12, "Verily, verily, I say unto you, He that believeth on me, the works that I do shall he do also; and greater works than these shall he do; because I go unto my Father."

THE POWER OF THE VIRTUOUS WOMAN'S HANDS

Throughout Proverbs 31 the word "hand" is used several times in reference to the virtuous woman.

- **Verse 13**: She seeketh wool, and flax, and worketh willingly with her <u>hands</u>.

- **Verse 16**: She considereth a field, and buyeth it: with the fruit of her <u>hands</u> she planteth a vineyard.

- **Verse 19**: She layeth her <u>hands</u> to the spindle, and her <u>hands</u> hold the distaff.

- **Verse 20**: She stretcheth out her <u>hand</u> to the poor; yea, she reacheth forth her <u>hands</u> to the needy.

- **Verse 31**: Give her of the fruit of her <u>hands</u>; and let her own works praise her in the gates.

The word "hand" actually has two different meanings in this text. One is the open hand, which indicates power, resources, and direction. The second definition is the hollow (cupped) hand, which is also symbolic of power. Power, is the ability to act or produce an effect, fulfillment, or reality. Whether the hand is open and outstretched to give, or cupped to receive, they both indicate power and have the ability to produce an effect.

The virtuous woman continually produces fruit and she is blessed in the process. She has an open hand that reaches out to bless and empower, as well as a cupped hand for receiving. She takes what she receives, plants it, and produces more fruit. It is seedtime and harvest at its finest! Picture it. While one hand is positioned to receive, the other is reaching out to be a blessing. It's a continual process. As long as you continue to plant, you will continually be in receipt of a harvest.

The first mention of her hands in the text is in reference to her seeking the raw materials necessary to produce fine linen. This particular verse references the cupped hand. Before she has the material in her possession she has a willingness to do what is necessary to develop it once she collects it. She has a plan of action <u>before</u> she receives it. She is not seeking out material to store it up or just accumulate *things*. She is gathering for the purpose of using it in a way that will yield more fruit.

Many of the purchases that women make are done so with no purpose in mind. We don't know *why* we bought it. We just bought it. We have no plan for it. We just saw it and thought, "Hmmm". We have no place to display it so we put it in a closet, in the garage, or a backroom until we figure it out. We have nothing that matches it. We just like it. It may not even be the correct size, but it was on sale and we had to have it. Sound familiar?

Remember, the cupped hand also has the ability to produce an effect, fulfillment, or reality. When you put raw materials in the cupped hands of a virtuous woman she will take it and produce something with it. Later in the text, it goes on to say that from the fruit of her hands she plants a vineyard. From the results of what she takes into her hands, she is able to plant something that continues to produce.

She starts out with empty hands, seeking wool and flax to make linen. But three verses later she's been so fruitful that she is able to buy a vineyard. Don't despise small beginnings. It's always exciting when God gives you a glimpse of something that He has in store for you. It's important to understand that you may not always be able to go from A to Z in a matter of days, weeks, months, or even several years in some cases. In the text, she didn't start with a vineyard. She didn't even start with an empty field. She started with raw materials. By making linen and selling it— from the fruit of what she began with, she planted a vineyard.

> *The virtuous woman continually produces fruit and she is blessed in the process.*

A virtuous woman is industrious. She uses her talents and skills to attain resources for her family. There are women who want to sit at home, do nothing, and let someone else take care of them. That is fine for someone with no goals, no dreams, no identity, and no drive; but not for a woman of virtue. A woman of virtue is a woman of purpose. A lot of women are seeking out men with high credentials that have a lot to offer, but they are unable to match or come close to what he is bringing to the table and I don't mean just money. They need to seriously consider what it is that they have to offer someone else.

It is shameful for a woman to browbeat and nag her husband for the bigger house, better car, finer clothes, and expensive jewels when she is wasteful, lazy, and not resourceful. What a disgrace to make him feel inadequate or that he is less of a man because the family next door *appears* to be better off financially. My question to her would be, "What are *you* doing to better the financial situation in your home?"

If you are fortunate enough not to have to work outside the home, then that is wonderful. I am in no way implying that being a homemaker is a bad thing. But consider what are you doing with your time? It is possible to consider, buy, and plant without having a "9 to 5".

What desire has God placed in your heart? If He placed the desire there, then He will also place the necessary raw materials into your hands to develop into something greater. Perhaps you are still searching and seeking, and that is perfectly fine. Make sure you are very sensitive to the Spirit and that you are watching and listening all around you. Sometimes we write too much off as a coincidence or freak accident. This is such an old cliché, but God works in such mysterious ways. What you think is a coincidence could be God leading you to your destiny.

I was terminated from a job that I thought was going to be the best job in the world and the beginning of a great career. I had just completed my undergraduate degree and was ready to roll on the fast track. It started out great, but ended suddenly after only four months and I had no Plan B. Just a few weeks prior to my termination my husband was telling me that I needed to devote more time to my writing and I agreed, but could never find the time. I was beginning to feel such heaviness about working and the amount of hours of the day that I was away from home.

It was blowing my mind that the same job that I was so energized and enthusiastic about just two to three months prior, was lulling me to sleep mentally. It got to the point that I dreaded going to work. I can recall driving to work the very week I was terminated and I told the Lord, "I don't want to do this anymore."

By the end of the week I didn't have to. Be careful what you say, your words carry a tremendous amount of power. Additionally, you can act out your thoughts and feelings without saying a word. I was not happy and it showed in my attentiveness, punctuality, and presentation. So, I was not completely innocent in the situation.

However, soon after leaving that position, people began to call me to assist with various projects, and they wanted to pay me. Initially, it seemed so silly to charge people and accept money for things that came so natural to me. I had enough projects going to keep me busy and we did not suffer financially. I was able to do things I was unable to do when I was working, such as, have lunch with my daughters at school, be home to greet my children when they got home, and actually have dinner at 6:00 in the evening. We had the opportunity to spend the summer together, which is something we had <u>never</u> been able to do. Also, it gave me the time I longed for to finish this book, develop future book ideas, and step into full-time ministry.

That "thing" that you do so well and that comes so natural to you could very well be God's gift to you, your very own raw materials to produce an effect, fulfillment, or reality in your life. In order to get to the next level and receive the "greater" that God has in store for you, it's going to require you to be faithful with the "few" that God puts in your hands.

In conjunction with that, it is going to require you to spend time in prayer, praise, and worship.

Lift up holy hands unto the Lord and reverence Him.

Lift up holy hands before the Lord as a sign of surrender, indicating that you are ready and willing to be used by Him and follow His direction.

You see, as long as you are following the hand of God, everything that you put your hands to will do nothing but prosper. Why? Because the steps of the righteous are ordered by the Lord and it is His pleasure to prosper you in every area of your life. The quality of the fruit that comes forth is determined by everything that you do while you're developing the raw material. That's why it's important to keep your hands and your feet clean. Prayer, praise, and worship are so vital. Positive confessions are key. "The power of life and death are in the tongue" (Proverbs 18:21).

> *That "thing" that you do so well could very well be God's gift to you.*

Proverbs 31:19 says, "She layeth her **hands** to the spindle, and her **hands** hold the distaff."

In this verse, the first "hands" mentioned refers to the outreached hand and the second refers to the cupped hand. A spindle is the straight, upright handle of an instrument used in spinning yarn. The distaff is at the other end and is the place where the finished product is collected.

Again, she is taking raw material into her hollow hand for the purpose of developing it into something greater. When you put your hands to the work of the Lord (on the spindle), He will put resources into your hand that will develop into something greater. It is the Lord who gives you the power to get wealth (Deuteronomy 8:18).

When I was pregnant with my second child, my first child was still in diapers. When I became pregnant with our third child, the second was three months old, but that's another story. We were not financially secure and I anticipated a money crunch even after I returned to work. There were some minor complications with the pregnancy in my sixth month. I was hit in the knee with a foul ball at a baseball game, after which I began to experience ongoing premature contractions. This left me with a lot of time on my hands, so to speak.

I began to seek out a second income that would bring additional resources and could be done from home. I got some information about medical transcription. I did the at-home course of study and finished it not long after giving birth. However, finding work was very difficult. I couldn't get any work-at-home jobs because I wasn't experienced enough. I had the equipment, the skills, and the school bill with nothing to show for it.

Six months to a year later I enrolled in a Hermeneutics course at church. During one of the lectures, my instructor was talking about Paul being in jail and how he continued to write letters to the church. I began thinking about the opposite scenario and being a blessing to people who are in jail who may not have access to some things that we so easily take for granted.

All of a sudden the Holy Spirit began to pour ideas and inspiration into my spirit pertaining to transcribing sermons on tape and mailing them to people in jail as a ministry. At the time I was also seeking ministry and how to utilize my spiritual gift. My husband was actively involved in ministry and I was feeling barren. I was taking care of the kids and ministering to him, but I wanted to do even more to have an impact on the Kingdom of God, but I didn't have a clue as to what I could do. This was about to change.

I began a Ministry of Transcription that gave me an opportunity to use a skill that I thought was good for nothing. It allowed me to touch people's lives that I would not have been able to under any other circum-

A Woman Any Man Can Love

stances. I have used that skill and training to do transcription for books and also to transcribe lectures from other classes to sell as study notes to students in the class. This Ministry of Transcription was the inspiration for The Virtuous Woman Newsletter, which was the springboard for Virtuous Woman Enterprises, Inc. (VWE, Inc.).

From the resources earned through the class notes and other ventures, I was able to invest in VWE, Inc. to reach out and touch the lives of women through the newsletter. I speak for several Christian women's organizations at monthly meetings. I preach at my home church and have spoken at International Leadership Conferences in Africa. There are plans to expand the ministry to include radio ministry, increase the availability of messages on tape or CD, write additional inspirational and instructional books for women, plan and sponsor conferences for men and women, and get involved in teen mentoring.

You never know what God will use to bless you with. The very thing that you think is a waste of time, or the thing that you feel is of no significance could very well be the gift that God has given you to be a two-fold blessing. It is a two-fold blessing because (1) it touches and enhances the lives of others and, (2) it is a blessing to you as well.

Finally, the virtuous woman stretches forth her hands to the poor, and to the needy. The hand that she stretches forth to the poor is the hand of power, means, resources, and direction. The poor refers to those who are depressed in mind or circumstances, including, but not limited to those with a lack of money. She has power and influence and doesn't mind coming to the aid of someone who has fallen. But remember, she only invests in those things that will produce more fruit. Therefore, she must follow the leading of the Holy Spirit regarding helping others.

There may be people in your life that could use your help, but the Lord may not release you to bless them or speak into their lives at the current time. This is where spiritual discernment is vital. As women, we are emotional beings and many times act out of an emotional response. But in order to reap a bountiful harvest, you have to be a good steward of whatever God places in your hands or invests in you by planting it on good ground.

As a result of stretching forth her hand of power to the poor, the second part of that verse says, yes or certainly, she reaches out her hand to the needy. To be needy is to be in want of something. It doesn't necessarily mean to be poor. You can be in need of peace in your life. You can be in need of a word from the Lord. You can be in

> *Everything that comes your way isn't necessarily for you.*

need of edification and a point in the right direction to put you back on track. Recall that the hollow hand is always in position to receive raw material that needs further developing.

Everything that comes your way isn't necessarily for you. Sometimes God allows you to be abundantly blessed so that you can be a blessing to someone else. The woman of virtue does not develop the material and give finished product. Instead, we see her empowering the needy to pull themselves up by giving them raw material so they can develop it into that which will produce a harvest and be a blessing for them.

I once worked for a Chiropractor who had a big heart and would sometimes not charge patients for parts of their care if they were unable to afford treatment. Not all, but many of those who received free care would not stick to the treatment plan, would be late and/or miss appointments altogether. The care had no value to them because they didn't have to pay for it. He later stopped giving his services away and created a "cash plan" for those that were uninsured, giving them a reduced rate for paying cash with a benefit of unlimited care for a certain time period. The people who paid followed their treatment plan and were less apt to miss appointments because it cost them something, which gave it value.

Many times people are just looking for a handout without working for it. This virtuous woman was wise in that she gave the needy something that they could develop and cultivate so that when the harvest came, it would bring them not only blessings, but also a sense of pride. This elevates self-esteem and self-worth. She transfers power, the ability to produce a fulfillment and reality in the lives of others.

As a result of helping the poor, those in a depressed state, the Lord will continue to bless you to be a blessing to those in need. This brings me to the final verse of the Proverbs 31 text, "Give her of the fruit of her **hands**; and let her own works praise her in the gates" (Proverbs 31:31).

This is in reference to the open hand of power and resources. The virtuous woman is blessed as a result of yielding her wisdom, influence, and resources to others. It is not necessary for the virtuous woman to be boastful and brag about what she does. She doesn't need to stand up in the crowd and give a listing of all of her charitable contributions, who she counseled when they were "going through", or who she helped that had insufficiencies. That which she does will praise her.

The word "works" is translated as actions (good or bad). Your actions, whether they are good or bad, will give a good view of exactly who you are. What you do and how you act will speak on your behalf without you or anyone else opening their mouth. In this case, her works were good and she gained notoriety by the good that she did with what she had. Make certain that your hands are giving and receiving that which is holy and acceptable to the Lord, so that the fruit that comes forth will yield the type of praise that is favorable.

It is impossible to escape the principle of sowing and reaping. God's word says, "While the earth remaineth, seedtime and harvest, and cold and heat, and summer and winter, and day and night shall not cease" (Genesis 8:22).

God operates by this principle, and has set a pattern for you to follow. In order for you to have fruit, you have to plant. What is in your hand and what you do with it will determine the quantity *and* quality of your fruit.

FOR YOUR SPIRITUAL GROWTH:

Self-Evaluation

1. Are you planting seed that produces good fruit?
2. If you answered yes, what do you do with your harvest when it comes?
3. If you answered no, as a woman of virtue and influence it is critical that you begin to invest in someone or something that yields good fruit. Seek God and WAIT for instructions.

This is an area that many start out strong, but it is easy to become distracted and lose focus. Don't dismay. Look to the Lord who is able to strengthen you, revive you, and get you back on track if ever you lose your way.

Prayer:

Lord, as an extension of Your mighty hand, first allow me to recognized those gifts, talents, and ideas that You gave me. Second, show me how I can use them to be a blessing to others. Further, I put all of my trust and confidence in You and am depending on You alone to lead me to the right people (to both receive and release blessings) and the right activities (where I can impart in others and see them flourish). Bless me Lord, so I can be a blessing to others. I will forever give You the praise, glory, and honor for it all. In Jesus' name, Amen.

CHAPTER SIX

LOOKING WELL OR EATING IDLE

"She looketh well to the ways of her household,
and eateth not the bread of idleness."
Proverbs 31:27

We have looked at several things pertaining to the Proverbs 31 woman: what it means to be virtuous, what the virtuous woman does, and how she is a blessing to others. In this chapter we will focus on the virtuous woman and her family.

There is so much chaos going on in the world today that if you are not firmly rooted and grounded in the Word of God, you will waste time and energy worrying about reports on the news or articles in the newspapers and magazines. Today we have school shootings, unknown viruses, missing person reports, and terrorist attacks just to name a few. These are serious matters and we should take caution, but not give in to fear for ourselves or our loved ones.

She is not afraid of the snow for her household: for
all her household are clothed with scarlet.
(Proverbs 31:21)

The word "snow" in Proverbs 31:21 comes from a word that means to be white with the linen clothing of the slain. As a virtuous woman, there is no need to be afraid of death and destruction for you, your family, or anything that you have built, physically or spiritually. Why? Because everything belonging to you is covered in scarlet (crimson), the blood of Jesus Christ!

More than anything else, your family, your friends, your business, your ministry, and everything or anyone you have relationship with needs your prayers. Prayer plays a major role in spiritual battle. I believe that many battles are won or loss due to the quantity and quality of prayer. Your family, your possessions, and anything or anyone that God has entrusted you with becomes covered by the Anointed One and His anointing through prayer (communication with God) and declarations (speaking God's Word over them).

Even if you have a friend or loved one who passes away, but accepted Christ, the devil hasn't robbed you of anything because that person will live in eternity with the Lord. It is vitally important that you live the life of a godly woman. It's not enough to merely attend church services and go back home week after week, unaffected and unchanged. Your life needs to be an example to those who have not accepted Christ or to those who have, but for one reason or another have gotten off-track spiritually. Life is much too short and too precious, and eternal life is far too important for you to live a mediocre Christian life; not affecting the lives of others.

Begin to pray for your friends and loved ones, both saved and unsaved. Pray for your business or your employer. Pray for your church (the leaders and the members). Pray for the lost, that they will accept Christ as their Lord and Savior. Share your experiences with other women who may be going through difficult situations that you also had to face. Let them know

Many battles are won or loss due to the quantity and quality of prayer.

that God will bring them through, just like He brought you through. Your personal testimony is the greatest witnessing tool you have!

If you begin to do this consistently, then you too will have the confidence and assurance in knowing that there's no need to be afraid for your family because they will be clothed in scarlet.

Not only are they clothed, but the Amplified Version of the Bible says they are doubly clothed. Psalms 91:4-6 states:

> **"He shall cover thee with his feathers, and under his wings shalt thou trust: his truth shall be thy shield and buckler. Thou shalt not be afraid for the terror by night; nor for the arrow that flieth by day; Nor for the pestilence that walketh in darkness; nor for the destruction that wasteth at noonday."**

There is covering by the redeeming blood of Jesus Christ and covering by the protection and safety provided by God. Whenever you receive a bad report, whether it is from a physician, the news, or a loved one, meditate on that scripture and regain confidence in the truth that God's word cannot return unto Him void, but it will accomplish whatever it is sent to do. That is the time to go into spiritual battle, using the weapons of spiritual warfare for the purpose of reclaiming what has been taken from you and your household.

Sometimes you can be so afraid of something that you begin to revere it and hold it in high regard. Be careful that you don't give the negative a higher place of reverence than God, the One who your trust should be in. Let those crazy superstitions and old wives' tales go. They could be hindering your spiritual progression and putting you and your family in jeopardy.

Proverbs 31:27 says, "She looketh well to the ways of her household, and eateth not the bread of idleness."

The word "well" in this context has several meanings. Among them are to lean forward; to peer into the distance; to observe; to wait. It carries the idea of behold; to look up; to wait for; to keep the watch.

The following section is my husband's summation of the virtuous woman "looking well" to the ways of her household:

In her search for guidance concerning her household and how she can stay motivated, she looks beyond men, and finds herself leaning forward in the prostrate position to receive direction from God that will keep her mind on her mission. Her prayer isn't just for the moment because she well understands seedtime and harvest. Therefore, she is assured that her today is covered based on her everyday consistency in seeking God.

What she is seeking and looking for are answers for the times to come. She is doing what she always does; she is PLANNING. The interesting thing to me is that she is planning in the spirit to get physical results. She is meeting with the Chairman of her board (God) to get insight as to how she can be a continued blessing in the eyes of her household.

Yet, because "well" also means to peer, (look intently) into the distance, we can also gather that she is looking for a serious response. So serious that she is putting extra focus in the way she approaches God. She is looking for answers for times that are coming. She isn't consumed with what didn't go right today or what may fail tomorrow. She has found a way to worship God by simply letting Him know that her trust and focus is for this very moment, obligated to Him.

The virtuous woman who looketh well has a very unique ability to observe in the spirit what the Lord is leading her to. This ability comes by way of her learning to wait before the Lord; allowing patience to have its perfect work in her time of worship before God.

> **What she is seeking and looking for are answers for the times to come.**

The virtuous woman isn't looking for a blessing. She realizes that she is a blessing. She is "looking well" to build upon that which God has made her to be. Yet, she had to choose every step of the way to be an intense seeker of God's face by getting on her own face before Him. Looking well, for a virtuous woman is her ability to go beyond the natural realm to organize in the spiritual realm the affairs of her house, as well as building upon her partnership with God (Pastor Anthony Banks).

First, she looketh well. The second part of Proverbs 31:27 says, "and eateth not the bread of idleness." Idleness in the Hebrew means, to lean idly; to be slack; indolence. Webster's defines indolence as disliking or avoiding work; idle; lazy. It also is defined as inactive or a slowly developing tumor that causes little or no pain. Wow!

One of the definitions for "look well" is to lean forward and the contrast to that is to lean idly. In both instances there is leaning taking place, but one is to God for direction and motivation and the other is to destruction. That last definition should really make you stop and examine yourself. Think about a tumor developing so slowly that there is no pain involved. By the time you feel the pain, the tumor has grown tremendously and is having a negative affect on everything around it. Could that be you?

I know that you may get tired, both physically and spiritually. Sometimes you have to step back, slow down, and rejuvenate. Be careful that you don't remain in "slow down mode". The words out of your mouth shouldn't *always* be, "Oh, I'm just worn out. I'm taking a break!" It is perfectly fine, and sometimes necessary, to take time off. However, you have to get back on the road to your destiny or you will become stagnant and begin to suffer from spiritual atrophy.

There is danger in becoming stagnant. You become ineffective in the Kingdom of God and a hindrance to others. To avoid work is to know that there is work to be done and instead of doing it, something else of lesser importance is done. I'm quite familiar with the process. For a long time I called myself the "Procrastination Queen". It is something I have to work at continually because my natural inclination is to wait until the last minute and then crunch.

I would always find something to do to avoid what *really* needed to be done at the time. I can tell you that it never ends favorably. I used to defend myself by saying, "I work better under pressure".

The truth of the matter was, I waited until the last minute and ended up scrambling. God won't put more on us than we can bear because we're too busy doing it ourselves. If you are guilty of this, it is time to STOP! You cannot be a blessing to anyone by doing things at the last minute and definitely by avoiding tasks at hand. Ultimately, important details get lost and the outcome will be the production of something that is as ineffective as you have become. I'm speaking from experience.

What I have learned to do is to take things one step and one task at a time. My biggest struggle at work and at home was that I had so many things that needed to be done that I tried to complete many things simultaneously and let me tell you, it only leads to frustration. In my quest and zeal to become this super virtuous woman, I was trying to take on everything, do everything, and be everything. I was doing everything and accomplishing nothing. I became ineffective in my home.

My husband said to me one day, "Why are you doing this to yourself. You're running around like a chicken with your head cut off."

At first I got offended, but he was absolutely right. I wasn't considering the Lord or my family. I just thought I had to do it all…RIGHT NOW! I had to pray and ask the Lord to show me what to be involved in and what to let go.

I was out of control and feeling absolutely helpless and pitiful. It was right about this time that I wrote the following letter to myself:

> *"I've failed the two most important people in my life, my Lord and my husband. People praise me. My employer, co-workers, friends, family members, readers of the newsletter (some of which I do not know personally) praise me. As King Solomon said, it is all vanity, meaningless. What*

good is it to be praised in the street by strangers, but lacking and deficient at home? Chores piling up; overdue tasks; minimal time with the Lord; swimming in debt; finances crippled; husband distressed; and children neglected. The Bible says the husband of the virtuous woman says to her, 'many daughters have done virtuously, but thou excellest them all.' Not, 'you have poor time management'. Her children rise up and call her blessed. They shouldn't be rebelling to get a few moments of attention in between mommy's trek from one uncompleted task to another."

Don't let this be you. If you recognize yourself somewhere in those lines, you need to ask God to help you. Even now, I continually ask for His guidance in setting priorities and handling matters effectively. Try it. God has given you the Holy Spirit to not only be your Comforter during bad times, but also to aid and assist you daily. How many times have you said, or thought, "I need my own personal assistant."

Well, guess what? You have one. God has so richly blessed you. Too many people think of blessings in terms of monetary value. God's blessings come in many ways. One of the biggest is the Holy Spirit. He is our liaison between heaven and earth. Having a healthy relationship with the Holy Spirit can mean the difference between being a woman who looketh well to the ways of her household and one that eats the bread of idleness.

FOR YOUR SPIRITUAL GROWTH

You know better than anyone else what the issues are in your home, whether you are a household of one or ten. Although you may not want to admit it to anyone, you also know the areas in which you need to make improvements.

Don't allow hardness of heart or lack of drive to remain in your life. It is a set up to take your attention away from the affairs of your home. As Jesus said to Peter, "Satan hath desired to have you, that he may sift you as wheat" (Luke 22:31). He wants to sift you because of your importance in your home, on your job, in your church and in the Kingdom of God. As long as you remain indifferent concerning looking well to the ways of your household (for whatever reason) the enemy's foot will remain in your door.

My word for you: Make the commitment to change and make better decisions. How do you do that? It's simple. You do it.

Don't over-complicate the process of change. The necessary ingredient in changing is to slow down. When you slow down in your thinking, you will slow down in your actions. Slow processing equals slow output. When you commit to change in a certain area of your life, every decision (big or small) concerning that area is crucial. Also, do not try to make several changes at once. Take it one step, or one issue, at a time. If not, you will get frustrated and stop the process because it will appear to be too difficult.

You are a pillar of strength in your home. Take the necessary steps to ensure that you are looking well to the ways of your household so idleness has no place to abide.

CHAPTER SEVEN

THE "S" WORD

*"Trust in the Lord with all thine heart; and lean
not unto thine own understanding. In all thy ways
acknowledge him, and he shall direct thy paths."*
Proverbs 3:5-6

Mention the word submission to a room full of women and you are sure to get a varying range of reactions. Single women may excuse themselves. Married women may raise their eyebrows. Older women may say, "Yes, these young women need to hear this." Others will just sit quietly and wait to hear what is said.

We're not together in a group setting, but you are certain to fit into one of those four categories. And yes, the topic of discussion is **submission**. Single woman, don't excuse yourself. Married woman, relax your eyebrow. And mature woman, this is for you too. Don't put the book down now this is the really good stuff!

Just as many well meaning men and women mess up the description of a virtuous woman, many are also incorrect in their definition and application of submission. So, I would like to set the record straight and set you free to embrace the term. Yes, embrace the term.

What I would like to do first is simply define the words submit, submissive, and submission. I want to do this because when women hear these words they immediately become offensive (or defensive). Most women automatically think about being dominated or controlled by a man. Actually, the act of submitting is much broader than the

> *The act of submitting is much broader than the husband-wife relationship.*

husband-wife relationship and affects your life on many levels such as work, church, government, social groups, associations, and friendships. Further, it is important that you understand that before you can properly submit to a person or anything else, you first have to submit to God.

> **The definition of <u>submit</u> is [1] to present or refer to others for decision, consideration, etc; [2] to yield to the action, control, power, etc. of another or others; [3] to subject or allow to be subjected to treatment, analysis, etc. of some sort.**

To submit is to counsel with a higher authority before acting, whether it be God, a spouse, employer, etc. It means to have the ability to compromise and/or yield to another's wishes. To submit also means that you give yourself for inspection or analysis, spiritually or in the natural. It's to *allow yourself* to be subjected to something. Be careful who or what you submit yourself to; there are positive and negative affects.

> **The definition of <u>submissive</u> is [1] having or showing a tendency to submit without resistance; [2] easy to teach, manage, or discipline; [3] yielding.**

To be submissive is a step further than merely yielding to another. That additional step is yielding **without resistance**. Do you remember when you were a teenager and your parents, teacher, or some other adult asked you to do something you really didn't want to do? Or, how about that great idea you presented at work or some other meeting, but the person in charge thought their way was best?

In each case, you may have submitted (yielded) to the higher authority, but did you do it without resistance? If not, you weren't truly submissive.

> **Lastly, the definition of <u>submission</u> is [1] the act of submitting, yielding or surrendering [2] the quality or condition of being submissive; resignation; obedience; meekness [3a] the act of submitting something to another for decision, consideration, etc; [3b] something thus submitted, as an article or photograph to a publisher.**

Submission is the **act of** (putting into action) yielding with the condition of doing it **without resistance**, which is the key. It is having a mind, heart, and spirit that is pliable and open to change. One definition for submission is, presenting something for approval, as in an article or picture to a publisher.

- Who is the publisher of your life?

- To whom do you present your situations and circumstances?

- Whose advice do you seek for approval of your actions?

In all actuality God is both the author and the publisher of your life. He's the photographer and the film developer. He is so gracious that He gives you room to be the editor and make changes if you so desire. It is called free will. What gets you in trouble is when you take your changes, additions, and deletions to an unauthorized publisher for approval. You need to have faith in God who knows everything about you and follow His leadership and direction. Doing so will land you directly into His will for your life.

So many people like to quote Proverbs 3:5-6, "Trust in the Lord with all thine heart; and lean not unto thine own understanding. In all thy ways acknowledge Him, and he shall direct thy paths."

I can summarize those two verses with one word: SUBMIT!

Submission has to be your foundation for an intimate and successful walk with God. How can you have faith and not submit? How can you believe and not submit? How can you be compassionate and forgiving, but not submit? How can you, "be kind one to another," yet not submit? How do you love your neighbor as yourself, and not submit?

The Bible is clear in Isaiah 55:8-9 when it says, "For my thoughts are not your thoughts, neither are your ways my ways, saith the Lord. For as the heavens are higher than the earth, so are my ways higher than your ways, and my thoughts than your thoughts."

Your "natural" way of thinking and way doing things are not in harmony with God's. I have mentioned several of my *natural inclinations* throughout this book and if you went back and found them all, you will see that none of them are in harmony with God's mode of operation. When you received salvation, there was no magical spell cast on you that erased all of the garbage you had taken in from other people, television, radio, books, the internet, and yes, even church. In order for true change to occur, we all must have a reconditioning or renewal of our minds.

I like the way my husband put it during a message he preached. He said, "God saves souls, not minds".

The only way that your mind can begin to be renewed (because it is a process) is by setting aside our personal agendas and yielding to God. Romans 10:1-3 is interesting. It states:

> **Brethren, my heart's desire and prayer to God for Israel is, that they might be saved. For I bear them record that they have a zeal of God, but not according to knowledge. For they being ignorant of God's righteousness, and going about to establish their own righteousness, have not submitted themselves unto the righteousness of God.**

Paul is not talking about those without salvation and who have no relationship with the Lord. He is talking about Israel, the church. After Jacob had his encounter with God and was changed for life by His touch, God referred to him as Israel. Paul's prayer isn't for Jacob, the trickster, but Israel, the changed individual. I found this passage of scripture to be interesting because he's talking about those who have been touched by God, but yet his prayer for them is that they would be saved! Saved from what? Saved from themselves.

We all must have a reconditioning or renewal of our minds.

Paul says that you may have zeal for God, but not according to knowledge. In other words, you can come to church, sing, clap, dance and shout in the aisle. You like to praise, but your praise is not enough to get you to the next level in the Kingdom of God. Yes, you're enthusiastic, but your enthusiasm is not in harmony or in agreement with true understanding. The problem is that you have not submitted yourself to God's word; therefore, you cannot receive that which is true because it clashes with your mental conditioning. You're still on milk and cannot chew and digest the meat. Hebrews 5:12-13 states:

> **For when for the time ye ought to be teachers, ye have need that one teach you again which be the first principles of the oracles of God; and are become such as have need of milk, and not of strong meat. For every one that useth milk is unskillful in the word of righteousness: for he is a babe.**

Again, he's talking to Israel. When Jacob wrestled with the physical manifestation of God in Genesis 32 he had not yet had a true experience with God. He hadn't submitted. He and his mother went about their own way to establish him, when God already had a plan for his life. He couldn't receive that "meat" (the fact that God had already established it, he couldn't see it) because he was still on milk (hadn't submitted to God).

I want to go a little deeper with this and use an analogy that I'm quite familiar with to make this relative, which is breast-feeding. When a mother is breast-feeding, the baby sometimes doesn't "latch on" properly initially and it becomes a wrestle. The baby will continue to struggle with the mother until he gets latched on to the source that will supply him with that which will sustain him. Once she is latched on, she will not let go until she is full.

In Jacob's struggle his opponent said to him, "Let me go, for the day breaketh."

Likewise, many mothers want to tell the baby, "Let me go. There are other people in the family I need to attend to. Surely you've had enough."

We need to be just like Jacob and the nursing baby and say, "No. I won't let you go Lord until you bless me. I won't let you go until I'm full. I've had an experience with you and it's good, but I won't let you go until you heal that broken place within me. I won't let you go until I'm satisfied."

Zeal is good. Praise is good, but there is so much more! After the praise, after the initial zeal, don't let go until you enter into worship. Milk is necessary and is just enough to get you to praise, but to enter into worship and the true knowledge of God it is absolutely vital that you submit yourself to God's word.

You can't truly worship God on milk, because while on milk you cannot even understand the deep things of God because your thoughts are not His thoughts. Remember Hebrews 5:13, "For every one that useth milk is unskillful in the word of righteousness: for he is a babe."

You are ignorant of God's righteousness as stated in Romans 10 because you won't yield and let go of the milk. At some point, the baby is broken and yields without resistance in order to move on to solids because he recognizes that the milk isn't enough to sustain him. Praise is wonderful, but without the meat you can't enter into worship and the true knowledge of God.

Having "the mind of Christ" begins with submission.

Submitting is the only way you will allow yourself to be open and receptive to God's way of doing things; and it's the only way you will let go of your way of thinking and natural inclinations, and truly take on the mind of Christ.

At some point, we have to yield to God's way of doing things and "renew" our minds because our thoughts are clearly not His thoughts. Neither are His ways our ways. That renewal process involves submitting. All of the time, you hear people say, "I'm a new creature."

Well, I'm here to tell you that if you have not had a change of heart and mind and have not fully submitted to God, there is nothing new about you. In order to put off the old man, you have to yield. Your metamorphosis will never be complete if you do not allow yourself to operate in submission.

Having "the mind of Christ" begins with submission. When Christ was here on earth, he still had to submit to God. Several scriptural references confirm this. Here are a few:

> **I can of mine own self do nothing: as I hear, I judge: and my judgment is just; because I seek not mine own will, but the will of the Father which hath sent me. If I bear witness of myself, my witness is not true**
> **(John 5:30-31).**

> **For I came down from heaven, not to do mine own will, but the will of him that sent me**
> **(John 6:38).**

Even to the end of Jesus' days on earth, He remained faithful, loyal, and in complete submission to God. He tells God in Luke 22:42, "Father, if thou be willing, remove this cup from me: nevertheless not my will, but thine, be done."

Jesus submitted to the will of the Father and went to the cross. It was not Jesus' will, but God's will. Because He gave Himself, yielded Himself, verse 43 goes on to say, "And there appeared an angel unto him from heaven, strengthening him."

You may be afraid to submit and totally "sell out" to God; giving yourself fully to Him because you know that when you separate yourself from the earthly, carnal things that you love (including some people), there will be pain and anguish. There are some things you simply have to let go of. Similarly, there are some relationships that you cannot continue once your metamorphosis begins.

However, grace (favor) is available to those who walk in submission to God and His Word (James 4:6). God will ensure that you will be strengthened. You are never alone. Although Jesus is no longer walking the earth and is seated at the right hand of the Father; He did not leave you comfortless. The Holy Spirit is here to aid, support, and assist you.

Some people already know what the Lord has in store for them, but will never see it manifest because of an inability to let go of their way of doing things. If you are going to be the virtuous woman that God has already made you, then you absolutely HAVE TO set aside pride along with every person or thing that exalts itself over the knowledge of God. Humble yourself under the mighty hand of God so that He will exalt you in due season (James 4:10).

Virtuous woman, submission is the key that unlocks the door to you obtaining the qualities of the woman in Proverbs 31. It does not begin with submission to your husband, your

> *Grace (favor) is available to those who walk in submission to God.*

pastor, your employer, or any other person. Submission begins with God. If you can submit to God, it is then that you can be led by the Spirit and those attributes will begin to emerge within and out of you. A woman any man can love has nothing to do with the woman (per se) and everything to do with her submission to God. Her submission to God opens the door to the grace and favor of God to operate in her life.

The following is my translation of Proverbs 31:30:

> *Favor is deceitful—because all of those who you think are for you really aren't. Beauty is vain—it is not lasting and you won't be able to use the physical to get what you want forever. However, a woman that fears (reverences and submits to) the Lord, she shall be praised—will shine and be celebrated!*

FOR YOUR SPIRITUAL GROWTH:

Think of an area of your life that you have not fully submitted to God. It can be relative to praying and studying your Bible; it can be praise and worship; or it can be an area of sin or disobedience. Whatever the case, pick one thing and commit to:

1. Finding out what God's word has to say about that "thing".
2. Once you find out, submit to God's word and apply it to your life.
3. After that area is in submission, move to another issue that needs resolving.

If you find it difficult to break yourself from undesirable behavior, contrary to popular opinion, it IS NOT a day-to-day process. When you're struggling with life-controlling problems, from the minor to the serious, it is literally a second-to second process. In any given second you can have a moment of weakness and make a split-second decision that causes you to do what you are working not to do.

Therefore, don't discourage yourself by making unrealistic goals, i.e., "I'm going to stop today, tomorrow, next week, etc." Instead, from one moment to the next, make up in your mind that you WILL conduct the affairs of your life God's way.

CHAPTER EIGHT

SUBMIT TO GOD AND TRULY LIVE

*"Humble yourselves therefore under the mighty hand
of God, that he may exalt you in due time."*
1 Peter 5:6

In the previous chapter we looked at submissiveness to God. I'd like to continue the topic of submission to God because, again, if we are not submitted to God then we will not be able to submit in any other area of our lives. I continue to gain ground on the issues in my own life. That is not to say that there are not times when I lose a little ground. Nevertheless, the journey and the fight are far from over. I must continue to press forward as God continues to perfect those things that concern me. I know it can be frustrating when there are areas in your life that you want to see change occur, but it seems as though nothing is changing.

What you have to ask yourself is, "Have I fully turned this over to God?"

"Am I submitting to God's word on this issue?"

"Am I *really* initiating change or am I holding on to this 'issue' for selfish reasons?"

Many times we sabotage our spiritual success. There's no one else to blame and unlike the phrase coined by Flip Wilson, the devil DID NOT make you do it. Whether your issue is food, drugs & alcohol, sex, gossiping, stealing, lying, partying, shopping, or whatever…if you're having trouble letting it go it's probably because you enjoy it and you are unwilling to fully submit to God's word out of fear that you'll miss out on something. Again—I'm speaking from experience.

It is a mind game that has been played on women since Eve in the garden. She ate of the fruit because she wanted to experience "something" that she thought she could not experience in her present state. She wanted to possess "something" that she did not think the man in her life could provide her with (or that God was willing to give to her).

The game has not changed. It is still the same. Women over-indulge in eating, drinking, drugs, and sex to "feel" satisfied and/or to alter their state of mind. Women shop until their bank accounts drop to fulfill a sense of stature or accomplishment. Women gossip and lie to make themselves look good and place themselves on self-erected pedestals. Women have ungodly relationships and affairs because they feel that either God or their spouse is unable to provide them with what they need, whether the need is material, physical, or emotional.

It's such a shame that women fall prey to this type of deceptive thinking because the fact of the matter is—if you are lonely and suffer from emotional distress, He has not left you comfortless or alone. Further, loneliness cannot be eliminated with things or other people. It has to be dealt with internally. Too many times, women are disillusioned that a man, a child, or even a job is the answer to loneliness. Your void can only be filled by and through your relationship with the Lord. God will ensure that all of your <u>needs</u> are met. Your trust has to be in Him, not in your own abilities, and definitely not in another individual.

What you do not consider while you are being deceived in your mind is that there are consequences to pay. My pastor once said, "It's a terrible thing to have to pay the piper and you have insufficient funds."

He is absolutely correct. Having said all of that, I would like you to consider the following passages of scripture:

1 Peter 5:6-10

 ⁶Humble yourselves therefore under the mighty hand of God, that he may exalt you in due time: ⁷Casting all your care upon him; for he careth for you. ⁸Be sober, be vigilant; because your adversary the devil, as a roaring lion, walketh about, seeking whom he may devour: ⁹Whom resist steadfast in the faith, knowing that the same afflictions are accomplished in your brethren that are in the world. ¹⁰But the God of all grace, who hath called us unto his eternal glory by Christ Jesus, after that ye have suffered a while, make you perfect, stablish, strengthen, settle you.

James 4:7-8

 ⁷Submit yourselves therefore to God. Resist the devil, and he will flee from you. ⁸Draw nigh to God, and he will draw nigh to you. Cleanse your hands, ye sinners; and purify your hearts, ye double minded.

Hebrews 12:5-9

 ⁵And ye have forgotten the exhortation which speaketh unto you as unto children, My son, despise not thou the chastening of the Lord, nor faint when thou art rebuked of him: ⁶For whom the Lord loveth he chasteneth, and scourgeth every son whom he receiveth. ⁷If ye endure chastening, God dealeth with you as with sons; for what son is he whom the father chasteneth not? ⁸But if ye be without chastisement, whereof all are partakers, then are ye bastards, and not sons. ⁹Furthermore we have had fathers of our flesh which corrected us, and we gave them reverence: shall we not much rather be in subjection unto the Father of spirits, and live?

It is so important that you submit and humble yourself to God's word. You will never experience the fullness, joy, or true life as a Christian if you do not. Whenever you attempt to do anything of significance for the Kingdom of God, you will quickly be reminded of your issues, which may cause you to do nothing because you feel unworthy.

> *God loves you so much and He wants to empower you to prosper.*

If this is the case, remember Romans 8:1, "There is therefore now no condemnation to them which are in Christ Jesus, who walk not after the flesh, but after the Spirit."

The key in that verse is the statement, "who walk not after the flesh, but after the Spirit." In order for there to be, "no condemnation", you must first resolve the issue. Not only that, but truly repent which means confessing your sin or transgression to the Lord and turning <u>completely away</u> from it.

God loves you so much and He wants to empower you to prosper. He wants your life to flourish and for you to have great success. But He will not do it if you are in constant rebellion to Him. As the Hebrews text states, "For whom the Lord loveth he chasteneth," but it also says, "be in subjection unto the Father of spirits, and live."

> **And this is the Father's will which hath sent me, that of all which he hath given me I should lose nothing, but should raise it up again at the last day. And this is the will of him that sent me, that every one which seeth the Son, and believeth on him, may have everlasting life: and I will raise him up at the last day.**
> **(John 6:39-40)**

You and I are joint heirs with Jesus Christ and heirs of salvation. As joint heirs we have the same privileges, rights, power, and blessings that Jesus has. In the above text he says that it is the will of God, the Father that you should lose NOTHING.

You lose nothing because anything that has died in your life will begin to be resurrected at the last day. The last day is point in time that you decide, "I've had enough," not with lip service only, but also in your actions. It is then that God will begin to restore and bring life to whatever it is that is dead in your life.

Not only will the Lord resurrect your "things", but it is also His will to restore *you* and give you abundant life, forever more. Make today your last day of being uncommitted to God's word. It is only in the last day that He will elevate you. It is only when you humble yourself under His mighty hand that He will strengthen, exalt, and establish you. Make up your mind, stand firm, and hold your ground virtuous woman. Don't be misguided or deceived in your thinking. Seek God's wisdom and instruction pertaining to the issues of your life and submit to it without resistance.

When will your last day arrive? Are you ready to gain instead of losing? Are you ready to be elevated? If so, submit to God and truly live.

CHAPTER NINE

SUBMISSION AND PURPOSE

"And I will put enmity between you and the woman,
and between your seed and her seed; he shall bruise your
head and he shall bruise his heel."
Genesis 3:15

We have been discussing the topic of submission, yielding without resistance. What I really want to do from this point on is tie purpose and destiny to submission.

You are so precious to me. It doesn't matter that I may not know you or will ever have the pleasure of meeting you. You are precious to me because you are my sister and we share common bonds, the love of Christ and the power of the anointing. Not only that, but we also share a common purpose according to Genesis 3:15, to crush the enemy's head with our seed. Your seed is that which God has implanted within you. It is your anointing. It is that special gift that God blessed you with that you had nothing to do with. Your seed is what God intends to be your ministry, your contribution to the Kingdom of God.

Of all the things on your "To Do List", keeping your foot on the devil's neck should be a recurring item. This is your purpose for any and everything that you do concerning the kingdom. The fruit of your gifts and calling should fulfill <u>that</u> purpose. If what you are spending your time, talent, money, or energy on, where kingdom work is concerned, does not fulfill or facilitate that purpose being met, you are merely spinning your wheels.

There are two examples in scripture that I will pull from to show the connection between submission and purpose. We will look at Sara and Jacob. First is Sister Sara. If you're married, looking to get married, or spiritually tied to someone, pay close attention. Sara made multiple mistakes in her old age, one of which was acting out of impatience. God told Abraham that He was going to bless him, and his seed. He told him that his seed would outnumber the stars; but He didn't tell him how He was going to do that.

When Abraham inquired in Genesis 15:2-3, God told Abraham that his seed would surely come from his "own bowels" and this would be his heir. After this encounter, God made a covenant with Abraham and Abraham trusted in the word of the Lord. Now, I'm sure that Abraham relived his encounter with the Lord with his wife, and shared with her that the Lord was going to bless him with an heir. Here was her mistake. It's the same mistake that women make today:

- God gives hubby a word.
- Hubby tells wife.
- Wife is excited at the "idea" of it, but things are moving a little slow, so this is her cue to step in and take over.

Initially, God only said that Abraham would have a son from his own body. Therefore, Sarah excluded herself from the destiny, possibly because of her age and because her womb was closed. So, surely God must have meant that He would have to place his seed in another woman. She acted too soon and did not wait for the rest of the

> *Don't move out on things too soon because you can't see how God is going to move.*

71

promise. She was impatient. Perhaps she just didn't want to receive his seed. Maybe she didn't want to do what it would take to become pregnant. It's possible that she did not want to put forth the effort of being close and intimate with her husband. After all, she was an old woman; perhaps the whole ordeal would be uncomfortable for her.

To solve all of that, in the very next chapter of Genesis she sets him up with Hagaar. In her mind, the promise would still be fulfilled. If Hagaar conceived, the child would still be from Abraham's loins. But she missed it. God wanted to bless Sarah also. But she wanted to take control of the situation and bring about the blessing in her own way, not the way God intended. There was more that God had to say. He didn't say that Sarah would give birth to the child until <u>after</u> she messed up and Ishmael was born. Following her error, God completes the conversation that He began with Abraham in Chapter 15. Genesis 17:16-22 (NKJV) reads:

> *16 <u>And I will bless her</u> and also give you a son by her; <u>then I will bless her</u>, and she shall be a mother of nations; kings of peoples shall be from her." 17 Then Abraham fell on his face and laughed, and said in his heart, "Shall a child be born to a man who is one hundred years old? And shall Sarah, who is ninety years old, bear a child?" 18 And Abraham said to God, "Oh, that Ishmael might live before You!" 19 Then God said: "No, <u>Sarah your wife shall bear you a son</u>, and you shall call his name Isaac; I will establish My covenant with him for an everlasting covenant, and with his descendants after him. 20 And as for Ishmael, I have heard you. Behold, I have blessed him, and will make him fruitful, and will multiply him exceedingly. He shall beget twelve princes, and I will make him a great nation. 21 <u>But My covenant I will establish with Isaac, whom Sarah shall bear to you at this set time next year</u>." 22 **Then He finished talking with him**, and God went up from Abraham.*

Towards that end, I have this to say to you: Don't move out on things too soon because you can't see how God is going to move. God told

Abraham that He would give him a son by Sara, and *then* He would bless her. Before God will bless the wife, (employee, spiritual son/daughter, etc.) she must first be willing to give birth to something that will be a godly inheritance for her husband (or person set over her). She must produce something that will be fruitful for him and seal his destiny.

> *Are you willing to do what is necessary to get pregnant and give birth to Isaac?*

Married ladies, you are in covenant. You are his suitable helpmeet. Pride must be set aside for the greater good of the union. You have co-dominion and are co-rulers. You may think you have the upper hand by being "your own woman". You may think you are merely maintaining your individuality and independence. But—the fact is that you very well could be blocking your blessings from God and hindering your usability in the kingdom.

If you are married and you find that you are waiting and waiting and waiting for the blessing that God promised you and it has not manifested—take a personal inventory. Are you willing to do what is necessary to get pregnant and give birth to Isaac? Do you believe that you are not capable of conceiving and giving birth because of this, that or the other?

You are no longer living under the curse, "Your desire shall be for your husband and he shall rule over you" (Genesis 3:16). The desire to be in control is a curse that was placed on Eve. Women today think it is a quality of strength. It is not. It is a curse.

God gives a vision for the house, whether that is the church house or your home. We want the people in the pews to line up with the vision of the church. But, why is there so much drama about wives lining up with the vision and destiny of their husbands? Your destiny is dependent upon your willingness to give birth to his inheritance. Then God will bless you. If your spouse is lost or lacks direction—don't ridicule him, pray for him. Do not emasculate him, instead, encourage him.

Also, don't be like Sarah and interpret the promise for him. Don't have the attitude that says—*I know you don't expect me to do THAT! Surely God didn't mean THAT! Come on now let's get real. I'll tell you what; this is what we're going to do...*

Sara literally gave her husband to another woman. When she did, she messed up and caused nothing but frustration in her home. Once Hagaar and Abraham produced a seed, Sara had no peace. Don't turn your husband over to someone else to give birth to what God intends for you to birth for him. Nor is it wise to withdraw yourself from the process of helping him to reach his destiny, causing him to seek out others to do for him what you were placed in his life to do; <u>and</u> what God has blessed and equipped *you* to do.

If you allow this, there will be no peace in your home. God won't allow you to have peace until you give up your way and your personal efforts to bring the blessing about. Don't get ahead of God or try to rush God. If a counterfeit is birthed through natural means, (not according to God's plan), it will cause misery in your life because you will see your husband enjoying something with someone else that you had absolutely nothing to do with. After you get into trouble, don't expect your husband to bail you out.

> **Then Sarai said to Abram, May [the responsibility for] my wrong *and* deprivation of rights be upon you! I gave my maid into your bosom, and when she saw that she was with child, I was contemptible *and* despised in her eyes. May the Lord judge between me and thee. But Abram said to Sarai, See here, your maid is in your hands *and* power; do as you please with her.**
> **(Genesis 16:5-6, Amplified Version)**

Isn't that something? She messed up and tried place the blame on him for how Hagaar was treating her. Not only that, but she tried to make him feel guilty for something that she did. It would be like telling your husband to sleep with your housekeeper to be a surrogate because you did not believe you could get pregnant. They sleep together, she conceives, and she mocks you because she is carrying your husband's child, the child of promise. Then, you can't take it. She has gotten on your last nerve and you cannot believe your husband is allowing her to treat you this way. Bottom line— you started it and you must deal with Hagaar, whoever or whatever that is.

> *He knew that I needed someone who would not be manipulated by female persuasion.*

Submission is a topic that I feel very strongly about. My husband is bold, says whatever the Lord drops in his spirit, and doesn't hold back anything! God really knows exactly what His children need. He knew the type of man that I needed to be my covering. He knew that I needed someone who would not shy away from delivering those "hard sayings". He knew that I needed someone who would not be manipulated by female persuasion. Even though I didn't know what a real man was, He knew how to match His virtuous daughter (in the making) with a true, mighty man of valor.

Was it easy area for me?

No!

Has it been challenging for me?

Absolutely! So much so, that I used to find myself saying, "Lord, why do you have to hit me so hard?"

God deals with me straight and sharp. A friend of mine gave me a nickname, "Hearer of hard sayings."

I don't mind those hard sayings anymore because I have learned that by submitting to the hard saying, God has been able to perfect me and smooth out some rough edges. Submission has saved me more times than I can count. So many women are being deceived into thinking that submission is a death sentence. I have to agree with them on that point. Submission will kill your flesh, but give life to your spirit.

To every woman who is praying for a godly, spirit-filled, anointed man of God—watch out! He is a special and rare breed, uniquely created for a virtuous woman. You have to have a submissive, pliable spirit and heart. I <u>did not</u> say timid, weak and mousy. There is nothing timid and weak about a virtuous woman. You have to understand that there is a difference between being submissive, being timid, and being overbearing.

Being timid will allow the enemy to have a field day with you. Being overbearing will put up walls between you and those whom God intends to be a blessing to you. However, being submissive is for your protection, will open the door to favor and blessings, and is a quality necessary to have a fruitful life with a mighty man of valor. If submission is not present, you may get the man but everyone in the house will suffer and be unhappy because of your attitude.

> **It is better to dwell in the wilderness, than with a contentious and angry woman.**
> *(Proverbs 21:19)*

> **A continual dropping in a very rainy day and a contentious woman are alike.**
> *(Proverbs 27:15)*

> **The contentions of a wife are like a continual dripping [of water through a chink in the roof].**
> *(Proverbs 19:13, Amplified Version)*

So, if you want the mighty man of valor, make sure you are willing to come forth and be found as a woman of strength, power, virtue, and one who demonstrates that she can submit—without resistance.

The next scriptural example of submission and purpose we will look at is Jacob and the night that he wrestled with a man. Genesis 32:26

Jacob states, "I will not let You go unless You declare a blessing upon me" (Amplified Version).

Jacob tried to bless himself, but it only left him in turmoil and without peace. Even though he had the inheritance, he had no peace because he secured it with his own hands and he did it deceitfully. Jacob came to the realization that the inheritance was no great prize because God hadn't blessed it. So he said, no, I won't let you go until you bless me. In essence, he was saying, *I tried doing things my own way and in my own thinking, and I've messed up. Please take this mess and bless it.*

God spoke a word when Jacob and his brother were in their mother's womb. He said the elder son would serve the younger, but instead of allowing the "due season" to come, Jacob and his mother decided to take matters into their own hands. Even though he received the blessing, he did not receive it with honor and he knew it.

So, what does this have to do with submission? When you are able to humble yourself, God will exalt you and there will be no need for you to put forth additional effort in establishing yourself. "Humble yourselves therefore under the mighty hand of God, that He may exalt you in due time" (1 Peter 5:6).

Three times in scripture Jesus says, "If you put yourself above others, you will be put down. But if you humble yourself, you will be honored" (Matthew 23:12, Luke 14:11, and Luke 18:14). In Jacob's case, it was not until he admitted who he was that he was able to truly receive from God. He did not let the angel go when he touched his thigh. Even afterwards he continued to wrestle with Him. At the moment when the angel of God asked him what his name was, Jacob had to stop and think about not only his name, but his nature and his character.

Jacob had "things". He had wealth. Jacob even had the woman of his dreams. However, Jacob lacked peace and true honor that only comes from God. Everything that Jacob had, he gained it through deception and trickery. He learned it from his mother and carried it with him after he left home.

There comes a time when you must stop fighting, humble yourself, and take inventory of your spiritual condition. Until you are able to do that, God cannot honor you and will not bless you. It is not an easy task, but as children of God, it must be done. You can have what appears to be a "perfect life" with the man, the home,

> *When you are able to humble yourself, God will exalt you.*

the finances, the kids, cars, and clothes; but it will all be unfulfilling and empty if you're lost and don't know who you are.

After Jacob was able to admit who he was, then the angel declared a blessing on him that changed his name and his nature. You can trick people and manipulate circumstances, but you cannot deceive God. Yet, people try it all of the time. God knows who you are and He knows your heart.

> **But the LORD said to Samuel, "Do not look at his appearance or at the height of his stature, because I have refused him. For the LORD does not see as man sees; for man looks at the outward appearance, but the LORD looks at the heart."**
> *(1 Samuel 16:7)*

It is so easy to look at our friends, relatives, and colleagues and point out their shortfalls and deficiencies. It's not so easy to place yourself under the microscope of scrutiny for self-examination. But God's word says, "For if we would judge ourselves, we should not be judged" (1 Corinthians 11:30).

Many times we know what our areas of weakness are, but we tend to push those issues further in the closet of our minds so they don't have to be dealt with. It's time to clean out the closet and deal with *you*. Other times, people are completely oblivious to any shortcomings and think that there is nothing wrong with them. And then there are those who know that there are some things out of order, but they feel that they are okay because the degree of their shortcomings is not as bad as, *some people they know.* Therefore, they do nothing because of a feeling of superiority over others around them.

> *It's time to clean out the closet and deal with you.*

If you find yourself in either scenario, you need to begin to pray and ask God to begin to search your heart and bring to the surface those things that are not like Him so they can be done away with. It really is a humbling experience and it is a huge step towards spiritual maturity that will bring you closer to fulfilling God's will for your life and walking in your destiny. God has an amazing plan for your life. Read this sweet passage of scripture and be reminded of your Father's love for you. Jeremiah 29:9-14 states:

The truth is that you will be in Babylon (captivity) for seventy years. But then I will come and do for you all the good things I have promised, and I will bring you home again. For I know the plans I have for you," says the LORD. "They are plans for good and not for disaster, to give you a future and a hope. In those days when you pray, I will listen. If you look for me in earnest, you will find me when you seek me. I will be found by you," says the LORD. "I will end your captivity and restore your fortunes. I will gather you out of the nations where I sent you and bring you home again to your own land.

FOR YOUR SPIRITUAL GROWTH

Your destiny is tied to the destiny of your spouse's (church, employer, etc.) in that your blessing (just like Sara's) will come as a result of you allowing your husband to plant a seed in you that you:

1. *Are willing to receive.* If your husband is a God-fearing man who you <u>know</u> hears from God, embrace the words that come from him. Don't fight against everything he says. You may look at it as him being manipulative and self-serving, but God calls it a way to bless

you beyond anything you can imagine.

2. Nourish it once you receive it. Spend time in prayer about what he speaks to you. If he is wrong and has missed it, it will be revealed to both of you and you both will know how to proceed from there because the Lord will guide you.

3. Deliver at the set time. See Gen. 17:21. God says at the set time, which is the time that **He** sets.

You have to ask yourself, what has the Lord spoken regarding my spouse's life (my church, ministry, career)? What is his destiny? If you don't know, you need to find out and ask God to show you where you fit into it and how you can help bring his destiny into manifestation. You will never experience true fulfillment or walk in what God has for you if you do not. Everything you attempt to do will fail if it is in opposition to, rebellion to, or not in line with his purpose and destiny.

CHAPTER TEN

A WOMAN AND HER PURPOSE

"And God said, Let us make man in our image, after our likeness:
and let them have dominion over the fish of the sea, and over
the fowl of the air, and over the cattle, and over all the earth,
and over every creeping thing that creepeth upon the earth."
Genesis 1:26

There is a principle in scripture called, The Principle of First Mention. This principle states that the first time that something is mentioned in scripture, it reveals something about the nature of that person or thing that is consistent throughout the rest of scripture. Nature refers to the indispensable attributes of a person or thing. In reference to a person, nature refers to those deeply imbedded qualities that cannot be done away with.

I thought it would be interesting to look at the principle of first mention where the woman is concerned. Genesis 1:26 is the first reference to mankind, inclusive of both the male (man) and female (man).

"And God said, Let us make man in our image, after our likeness: and let them have dominion over the fish of the sea, and over the fowl of the air, and over the cattle, and over all the earth, and over every creeping thing that creepeth upon the earth" (Genesis 1:26).

Here, we get some insight into God's purpose for mankind, male and female. Notice that mankind's "first mention" is together as a unit, a team. God was saying, let us make mankind to be a reflection of us. God is all-powerful, all-knowing, large and in charge. He is who He is because of His character and His nature. It was His intent and purpose for mankind to be just like Him.

I have heard people say that God is God all by Himself and He doesn't need anyone else to be who He is. This is true because everything is wrapped up within Him. Unlike man, God is spirit and has no deficiencies. He possesses all of the bravado and strength of the male man and at the same time the tenderness, loving, and nurturing attributes of the female man. We know from scripture that the male was made first and the Bible tells us that the female was made using a rib pulled out of the male.

Essentially, when God made the male, he possessed both male and female qualities just as God does. After all, God made him in His image. God formed the man, gave him a beautifully furnished and fully stocked home. However, since man was also part flesh, God said it was not good for the man to be alone. He was in charge and had full possession of the earth, but he was alone. Genesis 2:18 reads, "And the Lord God said, It is not good that the man should be alone; I will make him an help, meet for him" (*comma inserted for emphasis*).

It is in Genesis 2:18 where we begin to see why God decided to pull her out of the man. It is here that we get a glimpse of God's purpose for making the female. Too many times people run the words "help" and "meet" together resulting in a new word, "helpmeet". However, they are clearly two separate and distinct words. God was making Adam a <u>helper</u>, who would be <u>meet</u> (suitable, complimentary) to himself. In order for Genesis 1:26 to be true, the male needed a partner to co-exist with in order to have complete dominion. As I stated earlier, they are mentioned together as man (kind). They are mentioned together, yet they are distinctly different, but at the same time they are equal in power.

> *We are struggling for something we were created for.*

If true dominion is to take place as God intended in the beginning, mankind (male and female) has to work together. But, because sin entered the equation, an imbalance took place. Men and women don't want to share power and authority, which are the keys to having dominion. Without a balance of power and authority, dominion will never take place.

This is not only true in marriage, but it is evident in many arenas including the workplace and the church. There is a struggle for power everywhere, which is foolish considering God created mankind (male and female) to dominate—together. We are struggling for something we were created for. This would be like the rain struggling to fall to the earth or the sun and moon struggling to shine light, which is absolutely absurd.

Have you ever been on an airplane on a cloudy day? Notice that even on the cloudiest day or night, or even during the most torrential storms that above the clouds the sun is still shining and the moon is still bright. The reason they continue to do so is simple. It is because they were created to shine light and illuminate. Just like mankind was created to have dominion. The problem we face is that we have forgotten or have no idea who we are, whose we are, and why we are. We have let the clouds, the storms, and other external issues become a hindrance to us (mankind) having true dominion.

Yes, I know sin entered the equation, which threw everything off balance. I am aware of the fact that mankind became subject to the flesh and the wiles of the flesh after the fall. <u>BUT</u>, I also know that Christ cancelled the affects and wages of sin. Sin causes death (spiritual and physical). These are facts of life. But the truth is that as a child of God you do not live according to the flesh, but by the spirit. While it is a fact that sin brings destruction, be cognizant of the truth that it is the Spirit that quickens you (revitalizes, restores, and invigorates you). Because Christ came, you no longer live under the curse of sin and death caused by the fall of mankind (male and female). Instead, you have been made free through the law of the Spirit of life according to Romans 8:2.

My point is that the male and the female were created to rule and have dominion over their surroundings. Just because some external circumstances come about, they do not dictate, overrule, or cancel out your purpose. If God said He created you to share power and authority, there is nothing that can change that. Remember the principle of first mention. It reveals the nature of a person or thing and the nature of a person or thing is irrevocable and indispensable.

The only thing that can block it, clog it, or stop it is you not knowing or accepting who you are, whose you are, and why you are. You know whose you are. You belong to the Lord. We've peeked at why you are, to help rule. Now, let's consider who "woman" is. The actual word "woman" is first mentioned in Genesis 2:22, "And the rib, which the LORD God had taken from man, made he a woman, and brought her unto the man."

Now, this was after God made the other animals and birds in search of a helper for Adam. None of them were suitable or comparable for Adam, so God made Adam a woman. The word "woman" means opposite of man. We are opposite in nature, but equal in power, and comparable by design. God did not make the woman to give the man someone to rule over. He gave man the earth and animals, the sea and fish, the sky and birds to rule and govern with the <u>help of</u> the woman.

You may not be married, but remember that this is not only a marital issue. It affects us on many levels. Certainly if you are married, as a wife you are to be the suitable helper in your home. In the workplace, the employer-employee relationship is very similar to the male-female relationship. The employer will not survive without employees suitable for and adaptable to the needs of the company. The business will not flourish and survive. Dominion of the marketplace will never occur, leaving the company in "survival mode".

I experienced this on one of my previous jobs. I had to miss a lot of time from work. The time was necessary for legitimate reasons that could not be controlled. The circumstances causing me to be away took precedence over the needs of the company. Therefore, for a season I was not able to fully adapt to the needs of the company because of other responsibilities. Therefore, the affairs of the business suffered. It was not the "well-oiled machine" it normally would have been had I been able to dedicate my full time and attention to it. Things were being accomplished, but true dominion was not taking place.

In the church we have the pastor-sheep relationship. They both need each other to have dominion and operate with power and authority. Our battle is not against flesh and blood, but it is a spiritual battle. The pastor is responsible for hearing from God, ministering to, and instructing the sheep according to the Word of God. The congregation needs to be adaptable and pliable in receiving from the man or woman of God. Not just to hear a good message, but to apply the message so that change occurs. They need to be willing to share the weight and do the work of the ministry. The congregation should be in prayer for the man of God and for one another. Remember, opposite in nature, but equal in power.

So, it doesn't matter if you are married or single. As a Christian woman, you have power and authority and God expects you to share dominion and power in your home, on your job, at your church, and in any environment He has called you to be apart of. Being "my own woman" will not get you anywhere. He never intended for you to be independent. He created you and I to be interdependent so you can have dominion and be in control of the circumstances in your life (instead of circumstances controlling you). This is your purpose. Until you embrace submission, you will not have what God intended in Genesis 1:26.

You have to reach a place of maturity and recognize that the person or people you are fighting against are more than likely the same individual(s) that God has placed in your life for a purpose. The purpose is having dominion, sharing power and authority, being fruitful, and multiplying together. Don't miss out on your ultimate blessing due to pride and self-centeredness.

According to God's purpose for males and females, both have power and we are to share dominion. God gave the male power and He gave the female power. The power of the male is not greater than that of the female. And, sorry ladies, but your power is not greater than the male's. Concerning power, the difference exists in purpose and function. God's purpose is not for the sexes to compete for power, overthrow power, or to misuse power. He intends for males and females alike to utilize our power and influence collectively and in conjunction with one another to accomplish His will in our lives and for His kingdom.

You would probably agree that a powerful person is an influential person, and an influential person is a leader. You don't have to be a man to be a leader. You don't have to be the boss to be a leader. You don't even have to be a pastor to be a leader. A true leader in any group is the person(s) with the most power and influence.

This is where many women get into trouble because they can sense the power that God has given them, but because they don't know the purpose of it, they misuse it. Women are leaders in the home, on the job, in the church, the community, and the world. We are seen by many and positioned to influence those around us.

The word influence can be defined as the power of producing an effect without apparent exertion of force or direct exercise of command. Too many people think that power and influence coexist with boisterous and coercive. This is where many people, especially women, make mistakes in the quest to become a person of influence. They want and expect others to follow them because of some external thing such as a title, position, or even physical attributes. However, to be influential is to gain support and a following that appears to be effortless.

> *The power to influence others is deposited in you from the Lord.*

On a natural, carnal level, what is seen externally drives the power of influence. On a spiritual level, the power to influence others is deposited in you from the Lord. It takes wisdom to influence and we know that wisdom comes from God. I will even go as far as stating that wisdom is the vehicle that influence rides in. You have to be wise and show good judgment if you are going to influence others positively. This means that it is possible to influence negatively. Any woman can use something physical to produce a desired effect with not much effort at all. But, it takes a virtuous woman of God to utilize her power of influence on a spiritual level to produce an effect in her house and family, in her workplace, in her church, in her community and in the world.

Earlier I noted that we are seen by many which puts us in a position to influence those around us. For example, men are very visual. They are stimulated on many levels by what they see, externally and internally. As a woman, your power of influence can draw a man into a deeper relationship with the Lord, or it can lead him to destruction. It all depends on how you use your influence.

Please understand that if a man sees a woman and is physically attracted to what He sees externally, it is merely a temporary attraction and will not last if at some point he does not "see" anything of substance internally. The effect of the power of external influence is temporary. Proverbs 31: 30 says, "Charm is deceptive, and beauty evaporates." Once it does, there had better be something else there to keep his attention.

However, if a man is attracted to you on a spiritual level, that attraction is lasting. When he is attracted on a higher level he will trust you and yield his will and natural inclinations to your influence. In other words, he submits. When he sees how you carry yourself spiritually, it influences him. When he sees your intimate relationship with the Lord, it influences him. When he sees your dedication and commitment to the Kingdom of God it influences and impacts him to strive for the mark, not alone, but with your help.

> **Her husband boasts and praises her, [saying], many daughters have done virtuously, nobly, and well [with the strength of character that is steadfast in goodness], but you excel them all.**
> *(Proverbs 31:28-29 Amplified Version)*

You may be in a relationship with someone who does not know the Lord or who does not have a close relationship with Him. Please know that it is not your job or responsibility to "save him", that work is done by the Holy Spirit dealing with his heart. We have enough roles to fill without attempting to fill the role of Savior. Although, his relationship with the Lord is not your responsibility, you do possess the power to influence him towards righteousness and holiness. 1 Corinthians 7:14 says, "Actually, the unbelieving husband is made holy because of his wife, and an unbelieving wife is made holy because of her husband."

The word, "holy" in that verse means dedicated to God or set apart. He has been made holy, dedicated to God and set apart because of you. Therefore, you don't have to harass, belittle, or manipulate him into changing his life. Remember, influence is the power to produce an effect without apparent force or commands. In other words, you don't have to say a thing; let your life be an example. 1 Peter 3:1-5 states:

> *1* **Wives, in a similar way, place yourselves under your husbands' authority. Some husbands may not obey God's word. Their wives could win these men [for Christ] by the way they live without saying anything.** *2* **Their husbands would see how pure and reverent their lives are.** *3* **Wives must not let their beauty be something external. Beauty doesn't come from hairstyles, gold jewelry, or clothes.** *4* **Rather, beauty is something internal that can't be destroyed. Beauty expresses itself in a gentle and quiet attitude which God considers precious.** *5* **After all, this is how holy women who had confidence in God expressed their beauty in the past.**

There are many others around you who are also influenced by what they see in you. People on your job and those you associate with notice how you handle situations and they watch how you respond to what is going on in your environment. You don't have to walk around quoting scripture or wear a cross for others to know that there is something different about you and for you to influence them to want to know how to be more like you.

In dealing with women in the church, you especially need to be responsible with the power of influence. The book of Titus gives us instruction on how women need to influence one another. Women who are just beginning their walk with the Lord should be able to look to those of us who have been "in this thing for a while" and be encouraged, receive wisdom and impartation. We have the ability to draw them closer to the Lord or run them away by what they see in us and how that influences them.

Your children look at you and are influenced by what they see, especially in their early formative years. Right now, my daughters want to dress like me, they want their hairstyle to be like mine, they want to do what I do and say what I say. They see me on the computer, so they get on the computer and surf the net (quite skillfully). It was amazing to see them as early as age three go online and work the mouse better than many adults! They love to write stories. They even go as far as folding the paper and stapling the middle so it looks like the newsletters they see us prepping to mail. I overheard one of the girls say, "When I grow up I want to preach like mommy."

If I were a different woman, my influence on them would be different. Our oldest son is in his first year of high school and I can see how my relationship with him will have an effect on the type of woman he chooses as a life partner. He has high expectations. Influence is absolutely amazing.

> **"Her children rise up and call her blessed (happy,**
> **fortunate, and to be envied)."**
> **(Proverbs 31:28)**

The power of influence shapes and strengthens that which submits itself to it. You have the power to build up or to tear down. Virtuous woman of God, you are armed with an awesome source of power—use it responsibly.

CHAPTER ELEVEN

VIRTUOUS WOMAN, YOUR HOUR HAS COME!

"A woman, when she is in labor, has sorrow because her hour has come; but as soon as she has given birth to the child, she no longer remembers the anguish, for the joy that a human being has been born into the world."
St. John 16:21(NKJV)

A mother is defined as that which gives birth to something; is the origin or source for something. A virtuous woman is a mother in various forms. She may have children in the natural that she has given birth to. We have seen that she is business savvy, which means she gives birth to industry. Also, she is a spiritual mother in that she gives birth to the spiritual seed that God places within her.

As a virtuous woman, you are a mother-to-be. To be pregnant is to have an offspring developing in your uterus. The word pregnant also means to be filled. You may not have children in the natural, but God has filled you with a seed. His offspring has been placed in your spiritual uterus. That anointing is your spiritual seed.

An offspring is a product of its parents. It has the traits and characteristics of each parent. I can look at any of my children and I can see my traits, as well as my husband's in each of them. The same is true with your spiritual seed. It is carrying the traits and characteristics of both you, and its Father. Well, what do I mean by this?

God has impregnated you with the anointing, which removes burdens and destroys yokes. You have certain talents, or *gifting* some say, that come natural to you. These are those things that may amaze others, but you tend to do them effortlessly. Essentially, God puts His "super" with your "natural", resulting in an offspring that is su-

> *Without the anointing talent is merely entertainment.*

pernatural. He puts anointing (super) on your talent (natural). In other words, He adds the anointing to remove burdens and destroy yokes to your natural talent. Therefore, when you are subjecting yourself to His leading and are operating in your spiritual gift, it carries power and has impact on others and the result is supernatural manifestations.

Some people are talented in certain areas, but it is only talent. Without the anointing talent is merely entertainment. A virtuous woman is a woman who gets results. She affects the spiritual climate, and gets results in the natural. God has impregnated you with His anointing. He has filled you with burden-removing, yoke-destroying power. You are filled and abounding with it. Congratulations, you are pregnant!

Guess what? God fully expects you to go full term and give birth to the precious gift that He has given you. So, what will you do when your hour comes?

Just in case you are unsure, let me remind you of who a virtuous woman is:

A virtuous woman is one who possesses a strong spiritual force with the pattern and strength of a tornado. God created her to develop into a woman full of strength and power. Once she is fully developed,

she is well on her way to fulfilling her destiny. Others cannot predict her exact path. It may appear that she is moving about haphazardly, but she is tuned in to the voice of God and following His direction. Her power is likened unto a full-scale army. Through her resources of prayer, fasting, studying God's word and wearing His whole armor, she is able to go into spiritual battle with tornado-like winds, the force of an army, and come out victorious!

Labor and delivery in the natural has a striking resemblance to its spiritual counterpart. I will use my first two pregnancies as an example because they represent a good depiction of how many of us respond spiritually.

Anyone who has had multiple births will agree that no two pregnancies or deliveries are quite the same. With my first pregnancy I was both excited and a little bit afraid. I was excited that this living being was growing inside of me. I was excited at the thought of seeing, holding, and kissing my baby for the very first time. I was excited in anticipation of all of the firsts that we would experience: the first smile, first laugh, first words, and first steps. At the same time, fear set in because I didn't want to make the wrong decisions or take wrong actions in raising our child. I was also afraid of labor and delivery. What would it feel like?

Similarly, when we first give our lives to Christ and yield ourselves to be used by Him, we are somewhat naïve, excited, and scared. We are naïve in that we don't really know what to expect and what this new life will bring. We are excited because we feel revitalized, renewed, and are full of hope. However, in the midst of that excitement it is possible for fear to set in—fear of the unknown.

You may find yourself thinking, *Now that I have given my life to Christ, what does it really mean? How will this decision affect the rest of my life? What will be required of me?*

My first labor and delivery experience went very smoothly. Now, I am not saying that there was no pain involved because no matter what techniques are employed or what type of medication you receive, there will be pain. It just went very smoothly. I slept all day after I received the pain medication at around 8:00 in the morning. I would wake up every now and then and moan. My mother and grandmother were in the room with me and were telling one another, "This is the strangest labor I have ever seen in my life. I can't believe she's sleeping!"

At 9:00 that night I sat up wide-eyed and announced, "I have to push!"

This really should have been videotaped. My family and the nurse thought I was out of my mind because I had been sleeping all day and was dilating very slowly. The nurse very patronizingly said to me, "Oh, honey. I just checked you 30 minutes ago, you're only three centimeters."

I repeated, "I... HAVE... TO PUSH... NOW!"

She said, "Okay, sweetie. Let me have a look."

When she did, the look on her face was priceless. She started calling for help. She told one of the nurses to page my physician because the baby was coming. The doctor arrived and I was already in position and beginning to push. Fifteen minutes later I was holding my little girl.

The first time God uses you to manifest something it is such a wonderful experience. It is wonderful because you know that God is using you to do something wonderful and to impact His kingdom. The excitement builds as you go through whatever processes you must go through and watch the project develop.

The time eventually comes when it must be fully birthed and manifested. Pain is not only associated with giving birth physically. There is also pain involved in giving birth spiritually. You may experience emotional pain that comes from having to deal with other individuals. Not everyone will be excited about your spiritual pregnancy. You may even experience some mental anguish as you encounter some hard decisions that have to be made concerning God's will for your life.

> *When your hour comes, spiritually speaking, what will you do?*

Giving birth is not an easy or simple process. However, God is so gracious and takes you through a spiritual progression as you continue your walk with Him. As a new believer, He won't require you to go through the same experience as someone who has been a believer for several years. He builds our faith by beginning with small things. Once you have been faithful with those small things, He will do greater things through you. Whether you are a new believer or not, when the seed that God places within you manifests, there is no prouder moment.

My first experience went so smoothly that the second time I was very confident, perhaps a little too confident. My thought was, since it went so well the first time, the second time would be a piece of cake because I knew what to expect. When the time came to go to the hospital, I was cool, calm, and collected. I thought it would be just like the first labor and delivery.

The only thing that was similar was the fact that this baby, just like the first, was two weeks late and I had to be induced. I did not have the all day sleeping experience that I had before. It was quite the contrary. As the contractions grew stronger, it was evident that something was wrong. The baby was not positioned properly. She was positioned face first instead of the top of her head, which meant her shoulders were rotated improperly and with each contraction the pain worsened. It hurt so bad that all I could do was close my eyes and blow with tears streaming down my face. My husband rubbed my stomach, back, and held my hand, but there was nothing that he could do.

My doctor had me to get into some different positions in hope that the baby would shift, but it was not working. He phoned the surgical team to prepare for an emergency cesarean. We asked if he could wait just a little while longer because I did not want to have surgery. He agreed to 15 minutes and we waited. On a scale of 1 to 10 the pain was 50! I whispered to my husband, "I don't want to have surgery, but I don't know how much more of this I can take."

He got up and said he would be right back. I asked him where was he going, and he just said, "I'll be back."

Not long after he left the room I felt the baby move. It was a strong shift that felt like she did a somersault. I told the doctor, "I felt the baby move. I think the baby turned. I have to push."

I don't think he really believed me, but just like the nurse from my first delivery, he said he would check me and if the baby had not shifted we would have to proceed with the surgery. So, he checked me and yelled for the nurses to come in because the baby was on the way. He asked, "Where's daddy?"

I said, "I don't know. He said he would be right back."

He said, "We can't wait. The baby is coming now. Someone! Go find daddy!"

A few seconds later he came into the room with my sister and I was already pushing. He got there just in time to see his little girl come into the world and cut the umbilical cord. It was by far the worst pain I have ever felt in my life. But when I held my baby girl as the doctor stitched my broken flesh, the pain that I felt waiting for her to come did not matter anymore. We were looking at, holding, and kissing the product of our seed.

Similarly, God doesn't always move the same way twice. Just because He does something a certain way one time, does not mean that He will do it the same way the next time. Also, attacks from the enemy will increase as God begins to use you more. The enemy does not want you to walk in the fullness of what God has for you so he will make attempts to hinder you from giving birth to your spiritual seed. You must maintain your connection with the Holy Spirit so He can let you know when you need to shift and when to remain still.

When God is moving in your life and you are getting close to the manifestation stage, there will be times when even those closest to you cannot do anything to make your situation better. I am certain that if my husband could have done something to ease my pain that he would have. There are some things that you will have to go through by yourself to get what God has for you. Those that you love and those who love you dearly may have to step back for a season. They may not be available during a time that you think they should be there for you, but you cannot allow that to stop you from giving birth.

I later asked my husband where he went when he left the room. He said he had to go and pray because he didn't want me to have to go through surgery. There are times when the pressure is so strong that you can't pray for yourself. All I could do was lie still and sob because the pain was so great. I could hardly talk, let alone pray. Thank God, I had a praying husband. It is so important to surround yourself with people of faith and people of prayer. When God is using you as His vessel, attacks and painful times will come. When you have been knocked down, it is good to know that there are individuals in your life that will keep you lifted in prayer even if they are not physically with you at the moment.

My point in all of this is that there is sorrow, grief, and heaviness connected to giving birth. However, when you hang in there and go through what you have to go through you will see that it was well worth it. You may have to squeeze someone's hand. You may have to scream and shout. You may even have to suffer some injuries. During childbirth it is not uncommon for the mother's flesh to tear as the baby is passing through on its way into the world. It is not pleasant at all, but if the baby is going to come through, sometimes it is necessary for it to tear the flesh.

As believers and virtuous women of God, sometimes we need to have our flesh torn. I am not referring to your physical flesh, but your natural, carnal, fleshy desires. When you are being used in the Kingdom of God, your flesh needs to be moved out of the way. It is sad that most people think of sexual desires when the flesh is mentioned. Yes, the flesh does include sexual issues, but it is not limited to that alone.

A fleshy desire can be any desire given to man by God that is used in excess or inappropriately. Your flesh could be hindering you from birthing what God has filled you with. Your flesh, not the devil could be holding you back. But, when you submit to the Spirit and not the flesh, and keep on pushing—the baby continues to come through until it manifests. As you submit to the Spirit and push in the spirit realm, your "flesh" will be torn so your baby can pass through.

When the flesh tears there may be emotional or mental pain involved. There is pain because there are actions, behaviors, and modes of thinking that we attach ourselves to that are not in line with God's will for our lives. As these fleshly things are torn from us it hurts because they have been attached and adhered to us for long periods of time. When we begin to pull them away it hurts.

When I was in elementary school in the late 1970's there was a style of shoes that were very popular. They had a plastic bottom and a shoestring that went between the toes and criss-crossed up the leg. They were very similar to the shoes that are popular today, except they were plastic and flat. Well, we were told not to wear those shoes to P.E. because they weren't made for running, especially on the blacktop. However, my mom let me wear them to school and since I wore them to school I didn't want to take them off at P.E. They were my shoes and I loved them, so I wore them to P.E.

Not only did I wear them, but also I ran in them on the blacktop. Guess what happened? Yes, I slipped, fell, and went for a ride on the asphalt. I had a huge abrasion from just above my ankle to just below my left knee. The skin was completely gone and I was bleeding heavily. The school nurse cleaned the wound, bandaged me up, and called my mom to come get me.

The next day, my mom and grandmother were attempting to change the dressing, but there was a problem. The nurse did not put any cream or ointment on the wound before bandaging it. Therefore, the old dressing would not come off because it was stuck to the wound on my leg. When they initially began to remove it, flesh came off with the dressing. Boy, oh boy, did it hurt. Nonetheless, the dressing had to come off. There was no way around it. It had to come off so a proper dressing could be put in its place and it was going to hurt. They did some things to make it less uncomfortable, but there was no way to avoid the pain.

That story is an example of how we can get so attached to certain attitudes or behaviors that have been incorporated into our lives through ignorance or rebellion. You cannot hold on to those things and continue to move into what God has for you. You cannot operate in the fullness of a virtuous woman of God and continue to walk in the flesh. You will not give birth to the great things that God has given you and hold on to your way of thinking and behaving. It will be uncomfortable at first to pull away from certain things, but it is necessary. Don't worry—God won't leave your wounds exposed. He has provided a proper covering for you in His Son, Christ. You are covered by the blood of Christ. You are covered with angelic protection. You are covered by the Word of God. He will not leave you hurting. He will fill every void, heal every wound, and wipe every tear.

You should also know that God intends for you to have multiple births. If you have given birth spiritually once, twice, three times or more, there is more to give birth to. God is progressive. He is always moving and continues to exceed His greatness. God is not like man and gives you a wham-bam-thank you ma'am! He will not impregnate you and walk out on you. There is always another level to ascend to and God will be with you every step of the way.

When your hour comes, spiritually speaking, what will you do? Will you push? Will you press forward? Or, will you back away and abort the process because the pain and pressure is too great to handle? Don't stop when you feel your flesh being torn. It is a sign that the baby is just about to be birthed.

What a shame it would be to stand before God in judgement with your spiritual babies undeveloped in your womb. You will have to give an account to God for your stewardship of the gift and anointing that He has given you.

You *can* do this. A woman any man can love—one who commands God's ear and continued favor is a woman who is clothed with strength and honor (Proverbs 31:25). God created you to be strong. He put strength on you as a garment. You are wrapped and covered with the strength to overcome any obstacle that comes your way. You have the strength to push until you see in this physical realm what God has deposited within you in the spiritual realm. Just because you don't see anything with your physical eyes does not mean that growth and development are not taking place.

When you are pregnant, you cannot see the baby growing within you. You do not get to see cells splitting, tissue and organs forming, limbs emerging, and features developing. You can feel it moving. You can see evidence that it is growing as your belly gets larger and larger. You can even get a glimpse of the baby through the aid of ultrasound and other sophisticated equipment. However, it is not the real thing. But, the fact remains that the baby is growing.

You have no clue what is going on in the realm of the spirit. You do not know all that God is doing to bring it to pass or all that the enemy is doing to attempt to be a hindrance. You know that God has blessed you to be a blessing to others. You know that you have an anointing that will remove burdens and destroy yokes. God may even give you a glimpse of yourself operating fully in that anointing through dreams and visions, but until it manifests it remains a dream and a vision. But, the fact remains that your anointing is growing within you.

Be faithful, be obedient, be yielding, and push virtuous woman. Endure the pain for the season it lasts. Just remember that He will turn your sorrow to joy.

For our light, momentary affliction (the slight distress of the passing hour) is ever more and more abundantly preparing and producing and achieving for us an everlasting weight of glory [beyond all measure, excessively surpassing all comparisons and all calculations, a vast and transcendent glory and blessedness never to cease!], Since we consider and look not to the things that are seen but to the things that are unseen; for the things that are visible are temporal (brief and fleeting), but the things that are invisible are deathless and everlasting
(2 Corinthians 4:17-18, Amplified Version)

What you experience during the process is temporary. There is glory waiting at the other side.

EPILOGUE

This is a crucial time for women, spiritually. There is so much tragedy, adversity, controversy, and all out rebellion going on right now. I'm not talking about people operating in the "world system," but in the lives of God's children. There are women jockeying for position as the head of their homes... even in instances where there is a godly man present. There are older women giving younger women unwise and ungodly counsel. There are young girls in this country walking out of their houses wearing as little as possible for the purpose of enticing, not boys, (which is bad enough), but men. At the same time, there are young girls in other parts of the world who are strapping on explosives, blowing themselves up and others with them to further someone else's cause.

Examine yourself and consider what you will do and how far you will go to secure and deem yourself fit for the Master's use? What will you sacrifice so that God can use you to produce seed that has the power and ability to crush the devil's head? Now is the time to get serious about kingdom work. You are already equipped with all of the power and strength necessary to do whatever it is that God has graced you to do.

I want to conclude by posing to you the same questions I asked myself several years ago after hearing that New Year's Eve sermon.

Are you who you say you are? Do you practice what you preach? Are you a living example? Does God look on your life and say, *That's my virtuous daughter?*

I used to be one who thought that emulating the life of the Proverbs 31 woman was an unattainable goal and that it was an impossibility to be this woman. God and the lessons of life have proved me wrong. Not only has my mindset been changed, but also my life is continually being transformed. The more I look in my spiritual mirror, I see more and more of the virtuous woman that God created me to be.

The good news is that God is no respecter of persons. What He does for one of His children, He will do for another. He wants you to be restored. He wants you to walk in and operate in all of the power and strength that He has equipped you with.

> *What will you sacrifice so that God can use you to produce seed?*

Jeremiah 1:5 says that before you were born God chose you, yes, you to be His chosen instrument for His use. You were destined to be a virtuous woman of God with the spiritual strength of a tornado and power of an army. You are equipped with the necessary skill and ability to bring about change in your life and the lives of those around you. The fruit of your hands is blessed. The fruit of your body is blessed. Whatever you put your hands to will prosper. You possess the tools and weaponry to reclaim, restore, and recover anything that has been lost to the enemy. You are even powerful enough to rise above life's circumstances and walk into your God-given destiny.

You are a woman of great power and influence—a woman any man can love, meaning:

- A wife that any husband can praise.
- A mother that any child can celebrate.
- An employee any boss can appreciate.
- A friend that anyone can enjoy.
- A woman who is respected by everyone who knows her.

APPENDIX

CHANGING STAGES: A PERSONAL TESIMONY

This is a recording of the personal testimony of Minister Tresha D. Banks.

BEAUTIFUL BEGINNINGS

It was 1992 and I was a full-time college student, 600 miles away from home for the first time. I had my own apartment and worked part-time as a Chiropractic Assistant. I was doing well in school. In fact, I was on the National Dean's List with a 4.0 GPA. So, why would a bright 21 year-old young lady with so much ahead of her enter the world of adult entertainment? I can answer that in three words, I spoke it.

I grew up in a small town in Florida. There were 2 or three topless bars in town, but I had never given that a second thought. When I made plans to move to Atlanta, I remember joking with a friend saying, "When I get to Atlanta I'm going to be one of those nude dancers."

We joked about it, but I never thought I would *really* do it. Even though I wasn't serious at that time someone was listening.

My daughter came home from school one day at the age of five and said, "Mommy, the devil has workers and they listen to everything we say and try to make us do bad stuff."

If only I could have had that wisdom in 1992.

I let curiosity get the best of me. First, I spoke it and after thinking about it for months and months I convinced myself that it would be fun and a great college experience. So, one day I drove to a club not far form where I lived and spoke with the manager. He told me that I needed to come back on a certain night to audition and I agreed.

I was so nervous that I drank three shots of *something* before going on stage to take the edge off. When it was my turn I went on stage before a crowded room of men with my five-inch heels, thong bikini, and proceeded to dance.

Beforehand they told me to stay dressed the first song. The second song I was to remove my top and the third song I was to be totally nude. By the second song I had so much money in the garter around my thigh that all inhibitions were gone. I was on stage, the center of attention, and everyone loved (lusted after) me. I thought to myself, "This isn't bad at all. I can do this!"

And so I did. It was the beginning of a long road filled with dips, turns, slippery slopes, and dead ends. But, ironically, it was the dance stage that ushered me to God's platform.

OFF TO THE RACES

In the early days of my dancing career, I thought I was doing just great. I was still in school full-time maintaining my GPA. I kept my after school part-time position and I worked 2-4 nights per week in the club making very good money. Customers bought me drinks throughout the night which kept me "lively". Occasionally I would smoke a little marijuana before going to the club to loosen up and *get ready*.

I even got bold enough to try different clubs and alternated between different places. I saw young ladies do things that I thought was abso-lutely (and ironically) distasteful. I couldn't imagine how they could do the things that they did. How could they allow men to touch them? Didn't they understand that the clubs had "No Touching Rules"? I couldn't understand how a female could be so irresponsible and meet men at hotels or parties after leaving the club. Didn't they realize how dangerous that was?

I DO?

I met a man in the club one night. He seemed to be a very nice guy and after several months of him coming in to see me we began to date. More time passed and we were spending so much time together that we decided it was crazy for us to be paying bills for two places when we were always together. So we moved in together. But after a little while I began to feel uncomfortable with living together. It didn't seem right. I felt that if we were going to be together and live together that we should get married. So we began to discuss marriage and started making plans. We were married December 18, 1993, but it was not *happily ever after*.

I continued to dance for about three months after we were married, but it was beginning to create a strain on the marriage so I stopped. It was a difficult time because I hadn't saved a lot of the money I made and the loss of the cash flow made things tight financially. Overall, I thought things were going well, but I noticed that he was becoming withdrawn. Needless to say the marriage didn't last. Four months after our first wedding anniversary he came home after a "business trip" and informed me that he was having an affair.

I had already come to the conclusion that he was having an affair. When he said he wanted to talk I was expecting him to tell me that he was seeing someone. I was prepared for that. But, I wasn't prepared for the rest of the conversation. He wanted a divorce so they could get married. He packed his things and moved out that same night! I was hurt so deeply and very confused. In order to stop the pain I turned to alcohol and marijuana.

Drinking and smoking was an everyday occurrence for me. I didn't want to deal with the thoughts or the hurt so I kept myself numb because my reality was too difficult to deal with. I got drunk or high everyday because I didn't want to deal with the reality of my life. I couldn't handle the real world (my world) so I went back to the world where I could be whoever I wanted to be, where I could drink all that I wanted and get as high as I wanted to without anyone saying a thing about it.

I stopped going to church, quit my part-time job, and eventually I quit school also. I spent everyday of the next 10 months in an intoxicated state. I woke up with a drink in one hand and a cigarette and/or joint in the other (on some occasions with powder in my nose), and I went to bed the same way. Going back to my life as a dancer seemed appropriate at the time. I could live on autopilot. What I didn't know was that the second ride would have more twists and turns than the first.

Everything I previously saw in the clubs and said I would never do, I did. My life was dictated by money, men, and drugs. I got to a point where I grew unhappy with how my life was going, but I thought I had nowhere to turn. I had no family in Atlanta. I was too ashamed to call my mother or anyone back home in Florida. Everyone would be so disappointed and I couldn't bare the thought. So I continued my daily life.

DOES THE PAST ALWAYS REPEAT ITSELF?

In April 1995, again, I met a man one night in the club. His name was Tony. We were attracted to each other <u>immediately</u>. We were like a magnet and a piece of metal. As soon as I saw him I couldn't take my eyes off of him. He commanded attention at 6 feet, 5 inches tall, 250 pounds, clean cut, well-dressed, and very handsome. He was joining a group from work whose table I just happened to be sitting at. He arrived around 6 p.m. and stayed until closing time, which was 2 a.m. After talking, drinking, and many, many table dances we spent the remainder of the night (or rather morning) together.

We began to see each other off and on. We enjoyed each others company, no pressure, no questions, no responsibility, and no stress. We spent a lot of time drinking and doing drugs together. We were both running from our realities. He was a manager at his company and part-time hustler. I was a drug-using stripper. What a match!

Three or four months went by before we opened up to one another personally and talked about our lives. The entire time we had been seeing each other God never came up. I didn't know that he knew anything about the Lord and he didn't think I did either. Our lives were everything but living examples of Christ. But one night we began to talk about Christ and from that point on the Holy Spirit really began dealing with both of us. The drug activity and drinking gradually slowed down, but I continued to dance because of the easy money.

I continued to dance, but it wasn't the same. I began to become irritated and agitated at work. It was no longer fun to be there. I began to feel like I didn't belong there and I felt out of place. This was scary for me because I "needed" to be there to keep from going back to and dealing with reality. I began to drink more and more and smoke more and more to remain sedated and numb. A friend that I spent most of my time with introduced me to laced joints, which for me was marijuana with crack cocaine crushed in it. I was able to go to another level of "high". So much for reality.

YOU CAN RUN BUT YOU CAN'T HIDE...FOREVER

One night I was feeling very depressed and I did something I had never done. I drove to a neighborhood where drugs were sold, alone, at night, and bought some marijuana. I left there and drove to another neighborhood and bought the crack cocaine to mix with the marijuana. Then, I nervously and very slowly drove home, crushed the cocaine, rolled the joints and began to smoke. But, this time it didn't seem like I was getting high so I smoked it all until it was gone. Afterwards I just sat there on my sofa staring at the walls and looking around. All of the drugs were gone, I was definitely high, but it wasn't enough to stop the voice of the Holy Spirit.

I began to sob as I reflected on my life. For the first time since my ex-husband left I thought about the separation and had to deal with the feelings of hurt and rejection that I had worked so hard to cover up. It was a difficult night, but also a night of strength. I cried a lot and for the first time in a very long time, I prayed.

I didn't leave the club immediately, but as time went on I couldn't stand being there. I got a regular job and re-enrolled in school part-time. The next step was to get back in church. I visited World Changers Church in College Park, Georgia with Pastor Creflo Dollar and felt connected the first time I went there. I was so excited about the church and couldn't wait to tell Tony. He told me that before he stopped attending church that his membership was at World Changers and he had served in the ministry as well.

Things were definitely moving in the right direction, but there were some obstacles. For starters, in the time span between my awakening and finding a church he ran into some legal trouble and had to spend a month in jail and approximately 6 months in a work-release program.

I was enjoying my renewed relationship with Christ. I attended all church services and even invited my mother to come stay with me for a week during the celebration of the church moving into the "World Dome". I introduced her to Tony and she seemed to like him a lot (I left out his legal problems). I hadn't seen my mother in a while and we had a wonderful time together. That was February of 1996.

THE RIDE CONTINUES

In April of 1996 I discovered that I was pregnant! It was almost one year exactly after my ex-husband left and I stepped onto the roller coaster. I was 23, single, and having a child with a man who was under the thumb of the law.

Just for a little comic relief: My ex-husband called me not long after I learned I was pregnant. His marriage of 6 months was failing. The two lovebirds were getting divorced. He told me he realized what a big mistake he had made and wanted to know if I would take him back. He said he understood I was pregnant with another man's child, but we could re-marry and the three of us could be a family. I couldn't believe my ears. I very graciously and lovingly turned down his offer.

In my late teens I had two abortions within 18 months of each other.

The second one was just months before I was slated to leave Florida for Atlanta to attend school. I had healed from the emotional scars of that and knew that abortion was not an option for me. So, I called my mother and told her about the pregnancy. She was disappointed, but supportive which I appreciated. Tony was released from the work release program and we spent a lot of time together. But, after a few months I began to detect that something was wrong. Patterns and signs of drug use began to show up. I wanted so badly to be wrong, but I wasn't. We had spent so much time together doing drugs so I couldn't ignore it and he couldn't deny it. We talked about it at length and we were going to work through it, but I was very uneasy with the baby on the way.

Shortly after, my position at work was cut from a full-time position to a part-time position. I wasn't confident that I could depend on Tony because he was dealing with his own issues, so I called my "mommy" to come and get me.

In July of 1996 I was four months pregnant and moving back home, leaving the father of my child in another state (physically, spiritually, and emotionally), unsure of what the future held for us. He and my uncle and cousin moved my furniture and other belongings to a storage facility and I left Atlanta. Tony and I rode together in his car and my mother and other family members followed. I could not believe I was moving back home—pregnant, single, no job, and no degree.

It was tough seeing Tony leave to go back to Atlanta without me, but I knew it was the best thing for me and the baby because he wasn't stable and I had no support system there. The next year was a very emotional one for everyone. There were struggles, falls, and delays. The plan was for me to return to Atlanta once Tony was stable. Initially, I felt that "I" had to be responsible for making sure Tony stopped doing drugs and "got it together". I felt responsible for him and also felt that I had to "make things right" for the baby. I grew up without knowing my father and I didn't want our daughter to go through the same thing.

I soon found out what some women never realize, which is there is nothing you can do to personally to change a loved one. Nagging, bugging, crying, or lecturing doesn't work. What does work is love, encouragement, praying (giving it over to God), and yes, sometimes stepping away (tough love). It was difficult, but I had to do it and it paid off because approximately three months or so after Toniesha (Tony + Tresha) was born there was a marked difference in him. I was so excited about it.

On one of his visits we went to church and he felt a strong bond with the pastor at the church. He decided that he wanted to move to Florida instead. After changing his mind and stalling for months, finally on July 1, 1997 he called and said he was loading the furniture on a moving truck and was heading down. It was almost one year to the day that we had packed up and placed my belongings in storage and I moved to Florida. One year later, he was coming to join me.

When I heard the big moving truck pull up to my mother's house at 3 a.m. I jumped out of bed and ran outside to meet him. I was so thrilled to see him. The next day he got down on one knee and asked me to marry him. I said yes. I had found an apartment prior to him coming and secured it with a deposit so we paid the first month's rent and began moving items in. We were married on July 7, 1997 at the courthouse, no reception, no honeymoon. As a matter of fact, we left the courthouse, finished moving into the apartment and crashed!

The next morning he said to me, "I hope you're ready for this."

I thought to myself, "Sure I am."

THE TIDES BEGIN TO CHANGE…QUICKLY

Boy was I wrong about being ready. From July 1997 until today I have experienced more change and growth than I could have ever imagined. I knew that we would attend church and that our life of drugs and partying were over, but I had no idea that his commitment to God and pursuit of his spiritual destiny would be such a high priority. I thought we would have a nice little "quiet" life and we'd go to work, and go to church on Sunday morning and maybe attend some Wednesday night Bible Studies.

After a month I saw that he was quite serious. We were at Sunday morning *and* evening service as well as Wednesday night Bible Study. He quickly got involved in other areas of the ministry including personally serving the pastor. He became involved in outside ministries including drug recovery ministries such as Teen Challenge International and Healthy Choice Ministries.

His son, Anthony, from a previous marriage, who was five at the time came to live with us in September of 1997. I became pregnant with our second child and Loren was born in June of 1998. Just three months after Loren's birth I learned that I was pregnant again! Our son, LeNavince (a.k.a. Buddy) was born in July of 1999, just two weeks after Loren's first birthday. So, two days following our second wedding anniversary, there we were, a family of six!

In the interim Tony had gone through leadership classes at the Bible Institute at church and received his minister's license. I had started a women's outreach ministry, Virtuous Woman Enterprises with a monthly newsletter. It didn't stop there. In February of 2003 Minister Anthony Banks was ordained and is now Elder Anthony Banks and I received my minister's license and am now Minister Tresha Banks!

Virtuous Woman Enterprises, Inc. is growing and expanding rapidly. In October 2002 the ministry was granted tax-exempt status by the Internal Revenue Service. It was a major victory for me personally because I did all of the paperwork myself. God is continuing to show me different areas of ministry and ways to achieve them.

In April of 2003 I attended a major international conference hosted by The Apostolic Church of Pentecost International out of Canada. The conference consisted of a special women's segment and the Apostle/Pastor from Zimbabwe heard me present my trial sermon in the leadership class (he was visiting Pastor Glover) and insisted that I come to Africa to speak. The final day of the leadership conference was "Ladies Day" and I was asked to be the main speaker for this segment.

The experience was amazing. I was invited back the following year to not only speak at the women's segment, but to do a session at the main leadership conference as well. I had the opportunity to speak to pastors and ministry leaders from several regions in Africa.

Oh yes, and that Bachelor's Degree that was left unfinished in 1995 was completed in December of 2005 after 10 years!

Currently, it is the summer of 2006. We have tentative plans to move back to Atlanta in the summer of 2007, which will be our 10th wedding anniversary. We are preparing to start a church where we can minister to those who are lost and impart into the lives of others—making a "Change for Life".

I entitled this personal testimony, *Changing Stages* for a reason. I once stood on stage before "hungry" men (and women) and fulfilled the lusts of their flesh. But now, with a renewed heart, mind, and spirit I stand on a platform, on a stage before hungry men and women. But instead of fulfilling the lusts of their flesh, I am honored to be chosen by God to give them life! God's word is life and precisely what we all need to fill those deep voided places, **mend** those broken hearts, and restore us in every area of our lives. I've **spiritually** and literally changed stages.

Only God could have done what has been done in my life. Only God can take a drug-addicted, alcoholic, college drop out, divorced, ex-dancer, and single mother, and position her and honor her with such a wonderful life. It is an honor not a disgrace to share the experiences of my life with other women because it always results in encouragement and hope. I count it an honor to be able to minister to other women and let them know that no matter what their past was like, what their present condition is, or what they "think" their future holds, that they too are fit for the Master's use.

This is my testimony!

Minister T.D. Banks

Who is Tresha Banks?

Minister Tresha D. Banks is an anointed speaker and gifted writer who has an awesome testimony of the power of change that Christ brings when we yield ourselves to Him. She is a wife and mother of four children. She formed Virtuous Woman Enterprises, Inc., a women's outreach ministry in November of 2000, which has had national and international impact. Here is what others have to say about her ministry:

> "Tresha Banks is a powerful, fresh voice that God is raising up to bless His people. Her anointing is evident; and the clear, insightful way she opens up the scriptures causes the heart to burn. Whether speaking on women's issues, marriage & family or current events, she has much to say that is destined to be heard. I count it an honor to be her spiritual father."

> *Apostle William L. Glover, Senior Pastor*
> *Mt. Hermon Ministries, Fort Myers, FL*

> "Tresha Banks is a unique gift of God to generations of women that are in our society in these last days. I believe that God has and is calling her forward to bridge the gap between traditional women and contemporary women that are in our society. She possesses and operates in the anointing of Ruth while bringing the flavor of Deborah. She is a woman that can provide the wisdom and guidance of a matron and yet demonstrate the ability to plan and implement a strategy like a general. She is truly a virtuous woman for this season of transition in the Kingdom of God."

Bishop Michael L. Kirk, Bishop of Auxiliary Ministries
Independent Church Fellowship Conference International

"*The Virtuous Woman* is more than a newsletter. It's a model program giving positive contributions to women of the community, creating an opportunity for spiritual development and encouragement in the hearts of the reader."

Vivian Hill
WCRM Christian Radio, Fort Myers, FL

"Your teaching has truly been a blessing in my life, which allowed me to examine myself and has inspired me to feed other women."

Tamike Brown
Virtuous Woman Outreach Ministries

If your church or women's group sponsors conferences or retreats and would like to receive more information on Minister Banks, contact information is provided below. She is also available for one-day events, seminars, and luncheons. For more information, contact:

Minister Tresha D. Banks
P.O. Box 669
Fort Myers, FL 33902-0669
Web site: www.vwe-inc.org
E-mail: tresha@vwe-inc.org

About Virtuous Woman Enterprises

Virtuous Woman Enterprises is a women's ministry dedicated to empowering women to be changed for life through the word of God! Minister Tresha Banks is the Executive Director. The ministry has a long arm touching lives in the United States, Canada, and Africa.

MISSION:

It is the mission of Virtuous Woman Enterprises to reach out, touch, and empower women through the word of God; making a change for life in their relationship with the Lord, their families, their communities and the world.

STATEMENT OF DESTINY:

It is the destiny of this ministry to challenge women to examine themselves and their relationship with the Lord. It is our hope that while doing so, they will begin to read & study the word of God, not only to gain knowledge, but to apply God's principles to their lives to bring about life-lasting change.

Life-lasting change will cause them to come forth as true women of virtue, fully submitted to the Lord, walking in the power that has been made available to them through the anointing; bringing about positive affects for them, as well as everyone they come in contact with.

When true virtue comes forth, it comes with a powerful force fueled by prayer; fasting; studying and meditating on God's word; and fueled by the leading of the Holy Spirit.

It is at that time when women can empower someone else to tap into their own virtue and power; so that person can have the same positive affects in their lives and the lives of their families, friends, and associates as well.

Ministry Vision

Then the Lord answered me and said:

Write the vision and make it plain on tablets, that he may run who reads it. For the vision is yet for an appointed time; but at the end it will speak, and it will not lie. Though it tarries. wait for it; because it will surely come, it will not tarry (Habakkuk 2:2-3 NKJV).

VIRTUOUS WOMAN NEWSLETTER:

The ministry produces The Virtuous Woman, a women's newsletter which began November 2000. It is our desire for this publication to be produced on a monthly basis. The newsletter is a ministering tool used to reach as many women as possible with a message of encouragement, restoration, and Biblical instruction. Donations to the ministry support the newsletter's production and distribution. As resources increase, the newsletter will be published monthly.

SPEAKING MINISTRY:

Minister Banks is available for speaking engagements. If your church or women's group sponsors conferences or retreats and would like to receive more information on having Minister Banks as a guest speaker contact us at 239.246.8556 or email office@vwe-inc.org. She is also available for one-day events, seminars, and luncheons.

AUDIO MINISTRY:

This area of ministry includes a positive confessions tape (Daily Confessions of a Virtuous Woman); live recordings from speaking engagements, and pre-recorded topical studies for personal or group Bible study (coming soon). Tapes will be produced in the name of Virtuous Woman Enterprises and will be offered to interested parties through the newsletter, seminars/conferences, other marketing tools & word of mouth.

OPERATION IRRIGATION:

VWE, in partnership with GloveMinistries International, sends transcripts of sermons to individuals in jail, prison, or "work camps". If there is someone you desire to bless with transcribed sermons, send us an e-mail with their name, ID (if any), and complete mailing address. This is a FREE service and recipients are always richly blessed when they receive mail that is uplifting and encouraging.

"I have planted, Apollos watered; but God gave the increase" (1 Corinthians 3:6).

VWE INTERNATIONAL:

After visiting and ministering to women in Zimbabwe, Africa, the Lord impressed upon Minister Tresha Banks that there is a great need to educate, equip, and enlighten HIS daughters in other countries concerning HIS word and how to apply it in their lives.

This area of ministry will involve packaging teaching material, audio tapes, and booklets for distribution to women in churches throughout Africa. There are also plans to make annual visits to various African nations for seminars, conferences, and workshops.

There is a great need for support for this area of ministry to purchase supplies, packaging material, and postage for distribution to our African sisters.

VWE ENCOURAGEMENT GROUP:

The Women's Group will be a Bible Study/Encouragement Group for women who are looking for ways to strengthen their relationship with the Lord, their families, and those around them. Using the Word of God and other Christian resources as a road map, the VWE Women's Group will provide women with Godly wisdom to face challenges in their lives while giving them a safe environment to be transparent and open their hearts and hurts so healing and restoration can begin.

RADIO BROADCASTING:

The VWE radio show will be a 30-minute program dedicated to ministering to the spiritual needs of women, instructing and equipping them through the Word of God.

CONFERENCES AND SEMINARS:

The purpose for VWE conferences and seminars is to provide a "well" for the spiritually dehydrated to come and drink of the words of the Lord so they will be refreshed, renewed, and experience true change for life in their attitude with others, and develop a true picture of their position and power as a virtuous woman.

This is the Vision of Virtuous Woman Enterprises, Inc. We pray that you will join us in empowering women to be empowered to prosper and changed for life! For information on how to make donations to our ministry, call or write to us using the information below. Donations can also be made on our website, www. vwe-inc.org.

Virtuous Woman Enterprises, Inc.
P.O. Box 669
Fort Myers, FL 33902-0669
239.246.8556

E-mail: office@vwe-inc.org

Printed in the United States
73807LV00002B/217-549